Ancient Soparaka

Photograph of Mound known as Burud kot, Nalasopara, dist. Palghar.

Ancient Soparaka

Madan Singh Chouhan

Kaveri Books
New Delhi-110 002

First Published in 2017
ISBN: 978-93-86463-05-0

Published by
Kaveri Books
4832/24, Ansari Road, Daryaganj
New Delhi - 110 002 (India)
Ph.: 011-4707 2321
E-mail: kaveribooks@gmail.com
Web: www.kaveribooks.com

Laser Typesetting by
Aarati Computers, Delhi - 110 009

Printed in India

Acknowledgments

My study on Sopara (Nalasopara) begun in 2009 when posted in Mumbai circle as a Superintending Archaeologist in the Archaeological Survey of India and worked there till 2013. In 2010-11 and 2011-12 conservation and restoration work of the site under study was taken up by the Mumbai circle and during that time a complete documentation work was done which led author to write a book on this most potential and less known site of Maharashtra. From 2009 to till date, apart from Mumbai circle, I worked in Patna and Aurangabad circles of the ASI where I indulge myself in the study of Buddhist and Brahamanical literatures so that to enable me to understand more about Sopara or Suparaka and for that Archaeological Survey of India's libraries of Patna, Auragngabad and Bhopal circles contributed more in my research work for which I want to express my thanks to the officers and staff of the above said circles for rendering help in the research work. I would also like to thanks Sh. Rajaram Devekar, Conservation Assistant and Sh. Kailash Nath Shinde, Junior Conservation Assistant of Mumbai circle for execution of restoration work, documentation and collection of field information from the site.

The author would like to record appreciation and support of the other colleagues of the ASI Mumbai circles including Sh. Zulfekar Ali, Dy. Superintending Archaeologist (Now Superintending Archaeologist in Bhopal Circle), Sh. Gangadhar Korgaonkar, Asstt. Superintending Archaeological Engineer (Now Dy. Superintending Archaeological Engineer at Goa circle), Sh. Rajesh Chandanshive, Photographer and Sh. Subhash Pandit, Draughtsman.

I have had various discussions on this site with Sh. C. Dorje, Ex Joint Director General and M. Mahadevya, Ex Director of ASI which encouraged me to write a book on this project. I am thankful to both my senior officers for that support and advice.

My thanks are also due to the Director Science, Directorate of Science, ASI Dehradun specially Ms Shilpa Raturi, SAC for conducting sample investigation of brick, mortar and stone of this site and submitted their report in a record time.

Finally a word of appreciation to my wife Sumitra and daughters Eva and Trisha for their support and encouragement.

Madan Singh Chouhan
Regional Director
Archaeological Survey of India
(Central Region)
T.T. Nagar, Bhopal (M.P.)

Preface

Maharashtra is the third largest state and the second most populous State in India. The state varied in geographical and environmental settings and gifted with rich cultural heritage, of which antiquity dates back to the millions of years. Consisting of 36 districts in the state, has 281 protected monuments and sites of national importance under the jurisdiction of the Archaeological Survey of India, out of them 93 monuments are in 11 districts of east Maharashtra (Vidarbha), 76 monuments in 9 districts of central Maharashtra and 112 monuments in 12 districts of western Maharashtra under the administrative control of ASI circles namely Nagpur, Aurangabad and Mumbai circle respectively.

Spread in 12 districts of Western Maharashtra (Mumbai, Mumbai Sub-Urban, Palghar, Thane, Raigad, Ratnagiri, Sindhudurg Pune, Satara, Sangli, Solapur, Kolhapur) these monuments are of different categories like rock-cut cave, temples, terrestrial and Island forts, wadas and palaces ranging from early historic period to the colonial India.

The most important among them are the Buddhist Stupa at Nalasopara in Palghar district, famous Elephanta caves and Kondana Caves in Raigad district, rock cut Caves at Bhaja, Caves at Bedsa, Karla caves, Cave group of Junnar and Pataleshwar cave temple in Pune district, Kanheri, Jogeshwari, Mandapeshwar and Kondavite caves in Mumbai suburban district. Among the Terrestrial and island forts; forts at Raigad, Janjira and, Kasa forts in district Raigad, Shivaneri and

Lohagad forts in district Pune, Sindhudurg and Vijay Durg in Sindhudurg district, are noteworthy. Out of the temples, Shiva temple at Ambarnath in district Thane, Bhuleshwar Mahadev temple in district Pune, Group of temples at Velapur in district Solapur and Jhabreshwar Mahadev temple in Satara district are worth mentioning. Whereas Habshi Gumbaj at Junnar in Dist. Pune, Khokri Gumbaj in dist. Raigad, Muhammad Tuglaq's Mosque in dist. Sangli represents the Indo-Islamic architecture in the state.

Among the colonial monuments, the Portuguese remains at Cheul, Bassein, Sion and Korlai are praiseworthy.

The antiquity of Sopara can safely be traced back up to the early historical period when the holy Dhamma had become the beaconing light for the search of truth in the Indian subcontinent.

Sopara (Ancient Surparaka) was the main administrative centre of Aparanta under the Mauryan rule (322–185 BC) as it is testified by the discovery of the Emperor Ashoka's 8th and 9th Rock Edict at Sopara (present Nalasopara). It is also well known that the Emperor Ashoka (273–232 BC) had deputed a Yona Thera Dharmarakshita to propagate Buddhism in Aparanta after the famous Third Buddhist Council (250 BC) held at Pataliputra with Mogaliputta Tissa as its president. During the Satavahana rule (230 BC–220 AD) too, it was a busy international port and an important administrative centre which is further proved by its references in the inscriptions of Karle, Nashik, Naneghat and Kanheri caves.

From the archaeological and historical evidences, it is clear that Sopara was a flourishing town and an important trade centre since the Pre-Mauryan period to 3rd century AD and from 9th to 13th century AD. However, from 4th to 9th AD., there is no evidence of cultural remains and therefore, it appears that Sopara had lost its strategic importance in this period due to rise in sea level caused by the effect of siltation.

Present Nalasopara (ancient Sopara) has proved its archaeological potentiality by finding various antiquarian remains from here in the form of stupa, inscription, pottery, relic casket, coins, remains of temples and forts, bronze images and stone sculptures ranges from 3rd century BC to late historical period.

The attempt has been made by the author to add some new findings with the already discovered ancient remains of this area so that its heritage wealth could be highlighted among the archaeologists and researchers.

Contents

List of Figures

List of Plates

Pl. 13. A fragment of stone grinder is found from south-west corner of the main stupa.

Pl. 14. A part of sharpner is found near stupa no 4.

Pl. 15. The fragments of temple are found from the south-west corner of the main stupa. These are parts of vedibandha.

Pl. 16. An another fragment of the walls of the temple is found from the south-west corner of the main stupa.

Pl. 17. Stone Votive stupa.

Pl. 18. Unidentified fragment.

Pl. 19. A fragment of railing is found from the south side of the main stupa.

Pl. 20. A fragment of vedika is found, from the south side of the main stupa.

Pl. 21. A fragment of the walls of the temple is found from the south-west corner of the main stupa.

Pl. 22. This fragment of stone appears thaba of the vedika of stupa.

Pl. 23. Unidentified fragment.

Pl. 24. A fragment of temple with having grooves for fitting clamps.

Pl. 25. Unidentified fragment.

Pl. 26. A base for fixing thaba is found from the west side of the main stupa.

Pl. 27. A fragment of ushanisha of vedika is found from the south-west side of the main stupa.

Pl. 28. Unidentified fragment.

Pl. 29. Aushanisha of railing found from the west side of the main stupa.

1

Introduction

Sopara, present Nalasopara (Lat. 19° 25', Long. 72° 47') is a large village in the Vasai sub-division of a newly created district by the name of Palghar which earlier was in Thana district, Maharashtra.

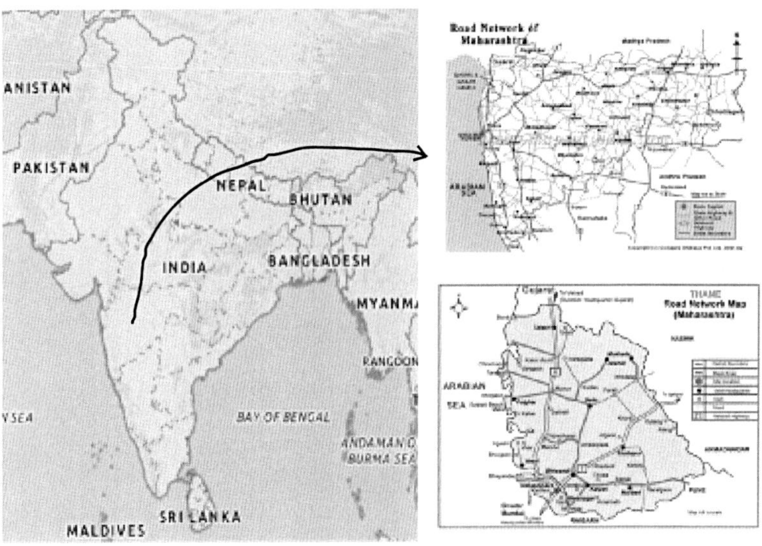

Fig. 1. Location map of Nalasopara.

It lies about 65 kms north of Mumbai and 7 kms south-west of the Vasai-Virar. The modern village stands on the side of the old Sopara. It lies on the west bank of a creek or back water which winds between the railway bridge on the Vasai creek and the Vaitarna. Though Sopara is no longer a port, but the old landing-place is still shown on a low mound about 50 m east of the Bhatela lake to the east of the town. The Old Sopara extends far beyond the present town. Being inhabited by the modern settlement the exact area cannot be made out, but the remains show that once whole the area of Vasai–Virar

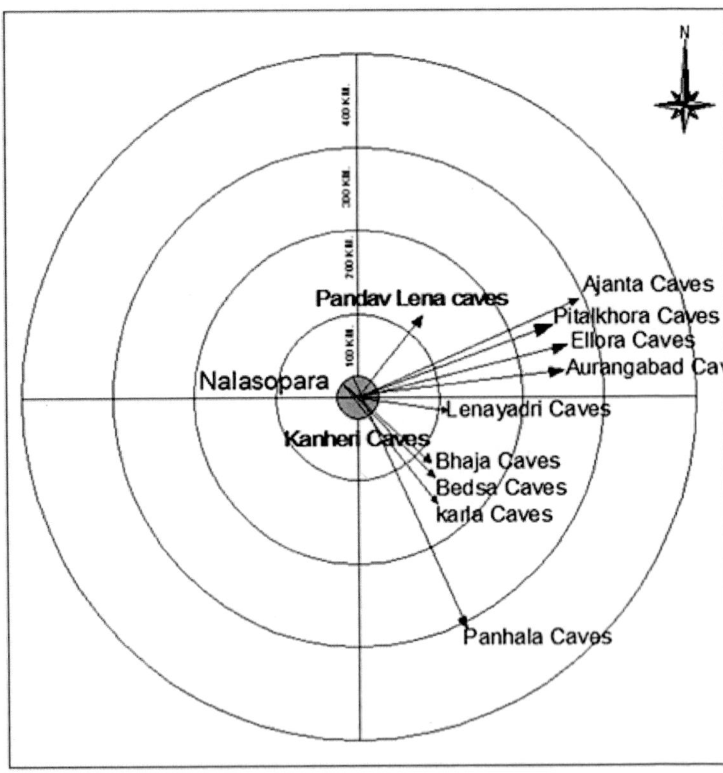

Fig. 2. Location of other sites from Nalasopara.

and present Nalasopara including village of Gas had been a part of old Soparaka and in ancient time it had an equal commercial status as today's of Mumbai. Presently, as in the modern town, most of the houses of old Sopara must have been built of wood, which when ruined leave no trace except their foundation plinth. The ancient remains are still visible over there in the form of sculptures, dressed stones, pieces of broken images, large old bricks, and besides these, the surest sign of an old city, an extensive provision for storing water. Of seven reservoirs the four largest are the Bhitela, Chakrila, Khare or Sirmoli, and Gas lakes, the last a great sheet of water 800 by 120 mts broad, with two cross dams. Besides these reservoirs or lakes there are three old water ponds and several old wells. The water ponds are Ramakunda, Pakarana, and Nogha Tirtha.

This site locates north of other Buddhist sites like Kanheri, Kondavite, Bhaja, Karle, Bedsa, Junnar, Naneghat and Panhale kaji caves whereas west of Ajanta, Pitalkhora, Ellora and Aurangabad caves and south-west of Pandulena caves of Nasik. All these Buddhist site are located from 50 to 400 kms from Nalasopara (Soparaka).

Being an important commercial centre in the ancient time it was located on the main trade route of India connecting Bharukachha- Simylla- Muziris from west to south and Junnar-Naneghat-Tagara-Pratisthana-Ujjain-Chaityagiri-Mathura from west to north of India and Soparaka remain continued in commercial and cultural prevalence from 3rd century BC to late historical period.

In the Buddhism, the meaning of Bauddha appertain to those who attained enlightenment and knowledge but upto some extent. The Sammyanka sambuddha has referred to those who attained perfect enlightenment and nothing can be hide from his unlimited knowledge. Aeons ago Dipankara was Sammyanka sambuddha prior to the birth of Gautam Buddha.

In the jataka stories a reference comes of a Brahmin named Sumedha and his wife Sumitra who were great devotee of Dipankara. One day on his visit, Sumedha lay prone on the muddy wet road whence Dipankara had to come across. In view that his feet should not come in the contact of muddy wet he laid prone so that Buddha could walk across his body. Seeing that echelon of devotion Dipankara predicted that after accumulation of perfection for many aeons, Sumedha would definitely become a Buddha by the name of Siddhartha Gautama. By saying that 'Dhuvam buddho bhavissasi" it is believed that these worlds of Sammyanka Buddha of that time reverberated through the skies and echoes again and again (Goenka, 2011,1).

After the aeons passed and time came when Sammyanka sambuddha has to take another birth in the earth. Before taking the birth an incident took place in Kapilvastu; a capital of shakyas whose king was Shuddhodana. In the month of ashada(July-August) there was a tradition that the king used to celebrate a festival for seven days along with his royal family members and common public. At that time, queen of Shuddhodana named Maya decided to celebrate that festival in very pious comportment by keeping fast for seven days and at the last day she rose early took bathe in scented water, bestowed the gift of 4 lacs of karsharpana (gold coins) as alms, adorned herself with all precious ornaments, ate choicest food and entered to royal bed chamber to sleep. Shuddhodana and Mahamaya came together and Mahamaya conceived after that she fell asleep and saw a dream that four guardians deities came and lifted her royal bed along with her and carried to kailasha mountain and placed her bed undera saal (Shorea robusta) tree thereafter their (guardian deity) wives came and took her for bathing in the manasarovara they bathed her, worn with fine dress, anointed and decked with perfumes and flowers in a manner fit to meet some divinity. Then a boddhisatva Sumedha appeared before and requested her that he want to take last birth on the earth in the womb of Mahamaya, would she consent for that as she said yes suddenly she awoke from the dream. Thus after ten months of that dream Mahamaya gave birth to Siddhartha in full moon of the Vaishakha (May- June) in 563 BC (Ambedkar, 2011, 18-19).

Gautama Buddha was so attractive and it is believed that on the basis of his physical attractiveness one who met first time to him could easily guessed that he was Buddha. On the astrological observation he possesses 32 attributes of a great human being on the basis of which he had been identified. Buddha attained perfection in the physical and religious/ intelligent embodiments. Even many of his devotees attracted at the first towards him due to his good-lookingness although he always denied physical beauty and stressed on religious/ intelligent perfection.

The childhood of Siddhartha Gautama passed smoothly but when he attained the age of 28 years till then he was married to Yashodhara and had a son Rahul, an important incident took place; the Shakya(republican state with capital of Kapilvastu) and Koliya (counterpart republic) arose to a conflict over the water distribution. The water of the Rohini river was used by both the Shakyas and Koliyas for their irrigation purpose. Every year they had to arose conflict on the issue that who should take water of river first and how much. On the age of his 28 years the same conflict arose again among them. Army commander of the Shakya called a session of the Shakya sangha (Association) to consider the question of declaring war against Koliyas but in that session Sidhartha Gautama who was till then an active member of the Sangha wanted to dispose off the issue peacefully without any war but his suggestions of solving the issue peacefully were not accepted and he was compelled to accept one of the three resolutions of the sangha; I: to join the force for war against koliyas, II: to consent to being hanged or exile and III: to allow his family to be condemned to a social boycott and confiscation of their property (Ambedkar, 2011:43-44). Siddhartha Gautam choose second option and abdicated his house and family and adopted exile.

Siddhartha Gautama adopted robes of recluse and became shramana (Buddhist monk). He left his house, wife, son, whole family and his country and after crossing anoma river on its bank he cut off his hairs, put off royal dresses and ornaments and gave them to his servant Chhandaka along with a horse named Kanthaka (Goenka, 2009:23). Thereafter he proceeded in to the region of Magadha (Part of present Bihar state) and reached first to Anupriya village where, in the amravana (garden of mango), he spent one week after that he wanted to meet Acharya Alaar Kalaam; a great saint of that time, but on the way he reached to Rajgir a capital of Magadha kingdom whose king was Bimbisar. On hearing this, king Bimbisar came to meet him. The king learnt that Siddhartha; a recluse was the son of his friend Shuddhodana of Shakya's, he requested him to give the life of a recluse and offered him a part of his kingdom but Sidhartha turned down that proposal and proceeded on his journey. He came to the meditation center of Acharya Alaar Kalaam and learnt meditation practices upto seven echelons. His next destination was to learn meditation from Uddaka Ramputta who was the master of meditation and had the experience of meditation technique up to eighth echelons after learning upto that stage of meditation technique Uddaka Ramputta had nothing more to teach Siddhartha while he (Siddhartha) wanted more to experience the reality of going beyond all existence, the state of permanent, eternal, deathless and immortal and for that he took another saunter from there for the search of enlightenment and he reached Uruvela; present Boddhgaya in Bihar and a place which was considered most appropriate place for meditation during those days. In those days there was also a belief that purification of mind, eternal state can be only achieved through torturing the body by various ways like by observing severe austerities, starving and remaining in adverse climate etc. Shramana Siddhartha followed that path for 6 years but failed to attain the ultimate destiny, thereafter he abdicated that severe path and started partaking of food, although by doing so his five companions who were following sever austerity along with him became disappointed of him and left his company by thinking that Siddharha had gone astray from the path and he would not achieve enlightenment (Goenka, 2011: 15-20).

At last Siddhartha remained alone and sat under a Vatavriksha tree (Ficus benghalensis) near the Sena village on the bank of Niranjana river for meditation. In that village a rich person named Senani had a daughter named Sujata who was the great worshiper of that Vatavriksha for long time. This time too, she wanted to offer worship and cooked a delicious porridge to offer the sacred tree but when reached there she saw an ascetic following mediation under the tree, the porridge which she brought to offer the tree gave to ascetic Siddhartha. That offering of porridge to Siddhartha is considered to be of great significance because that was the last meal had by him and after having that meal Siddhartha became Gautama Buddha as attained enlightenment. Thus in the age of 29 years (534 BC) Gautama Buddha abdicated his home, attained enlightenment in 36 years (528 BC) and preached dhamma(Baudha religion) for 45 years and at last in the age of 80 years (483 BC) took parinirvan at Kushinagara(Sankrityayana,1952:5-7).

After the death (parinirvana) of Gautama Buddha one incident took place. There was an aged person named Subhadra who after seeing the mourns of the people on the death of the Buddha he was shouting with loud addressing insidiously that 'mourn no more', Now everyone is free from the control of Tathagata (Goutama Buddha) son will now not depart to his father, father will not depart to his son, husband will not depart to his wife and wife will not depart to her husband. We shall no mere be worried with "this is allowable' and 'that is not allowable" and so on... By seeing that Kasyapa had numbed. He thought that within this short period after the death of Tathgata that sort of opinions had been created among the people, in future it may go very aversively among the public if conception of Buddhism were not disseminated properly. For that he decided to organize a council wherein preaching of Tathagata made earlier at different occasions could be explain and narrated so that their real purpose for the benefit of the public could be emphasized. In view to achieve that purpose, the first synod was conceptualized and decided.

The roles of synods or councils are quite significant in diversifying the Buddhism and in every synod something emerged out new for the adherent to the religion. First of all work of compilation of Tripitakas(Sutra, Vinaya and Abhidharma) were undertaken in hands by the eminent and learned monks. Of them Sutra was compiled by Ananda, Vinaya by Upali and Abhidharma by great Kashyapa. These three main parts of the sect were rehearsed among the prominent ascetics and monks under the supervision of chief monks and thereafter some new and old credence were added and omitted after the concurrence of the all.

In the first synod, which were held after the parinirvana of Shakya Buddha at Kushinagara and place decided for it was saptaparni caves at Rajgriha under the able guidance and supervision of Kashyapa in 543 BC. Prior to that occasion, a huge preparation was made by the ascetic community and spent whole of that month in repairing their viharas of Rajgriha (Cunningham,1854,57).

During the time of Sidhartha Gautama there was no system of worship in prevalence. He used to move one place to other with disciples to preach people about dhamma. He tried to motivate people for acquiring real knowledge. After his death, the triple gems of Buddhism; Buddha, Dhamma and Sangha got their own shapes of belief and Buddha had worshipped symbolically thereafter formation of sculptures, dhamma bifurcated into Hinayana, Mahayana and in Vajrayana and sangha were headed by those pioneers who believed in concept of Hinayana, Mahayana and Vajrayana schools. The school of Buddhism later on expanded in India and then subsequently, throughout the world. However, it was at the time of the Ashoka; Mauryan emperor, that Buddhism took a pace to reach its height. Ashoka after Kalinga war, decided to follow the path of non-violence and converted to Buddhism. He promoted the doctrines of Buddhism not only in his empire as Dhamma but in other regions as well. It was his promotional campaign that led to the construction of the Buddhist religious monasteries and stupas, which further facilitated the spread of Buddhism in countries like Sri Lanka, Tibet, China and Japan.

Out of many Buddhist site in India, Soparaka was one associated not directly to the Gautama Buddha but to the Soparaka; previous birth of Buddha who came here and offered remains of nails and hairs to his woman devotee to built a temple here. In a site (Mound locally known as Burud Rajacha Kot) a fragment of Bowl had recovered by Bhagwanlal Indraji in 1882 excavation which he claimed for it a part of Buddha bowl. If viewed from that perspective, this site and place Nalasopara are archaeologically quite potential.

2

Backdrop

Reference of Aparanta

In the Manual of Buddhism, Spencer Hardy has written that "the third journey of Buddha to Cylon was made in the eighth year after he had received Buddhaship. At the request of the priests of Sunaparantaka he entered the golden palanquin presented by the guardian devas alongwith 500 arahantas and went to the hall built by some merchants called chandana mandala in the forest of Mulu in the region called Sunaparantaka, where he preached to those who were present, remaining there several days. After this, at the request of Punna, he went to the town of Soparaka where many merchants were congregated; and to them also he delivered a discourse. From this place, on his way to sewet he went to Nirmada river at the request of naga king of the same name; and at this place he partook of food presented by the nagas to whom he preached and gave the benefit of the three-fold protective formulary. In compliance with the earnest entreaty of the naga king he left an imprint of his foot on the bank of the river in the midst of sandy desert, on a spot that is occasionally covered by the waves. This impression may still be seen in the Yona country at a place where the waves strike upon a sand hill and they again retire. It is only on the retiring of the waves that the mark of the foot can be seen. From the river, Gautama went to the rock Sachabadha, upon the summit of which at the request of same name he made an impression of his foot in clay. From the rock Sachabadha, Buddha came to Cylon (Hardy,1853:209-13).

In the old texts Aparanta or Sunaparanta or Sunaparantaka was a region of the western part of India wherein Soparaka was an important commercial town. In the Arthashashtra of Kautilya a list of hides and furs had described which provide information that during Maurya period Aparanta was famous and chief center for cotton products. Besides Aparanta other centers was Mathura, Kashi, Kalinga, Bengal, Vamsha (kaushambi) and Mahishamati (Today's Mahesar near Khandwa in Madhya Pradesh).

After the third synod of Buddhist, the monks converted people of Kashmir, Gandhara, China, Chilata (Kirata), Toshali, Vanga, Vanavasi, Yavana, Damidha, Tambraparni and Aparanta to Buddhism. In the 2nd century AD the power on Aparanta including Baroach was vice versa shifted among Satavahana and Shakas. At the early part of the century it was under the Control of Nahapana which later on went into the hand of Gautamiputra Satakarni (Motichandra,1977: 87-104).

Reference on Soparaka

"During illness, marriage, birth of child and setting out of journey men performs many ceremonies. The ceremonies should be performed but those kind of ceremonies are not so fruitful comparatively to those where courtesy to slaves, servants, reverence to elders, gentleness to animals, liberty to brahamanas and shramanas are done". (Ashokan inscription found from Nalasopara).

IXth Ashokan edict displayed at Chhatrapati Shivaji Maharaj Vastu Sangrahalaya, Mumbai.

THE IXTH ASHOKAN EDICT

Sopara, Maharashtra, 3rd Century B.C.

Sopara, (ancient Shurparaka) was an important port city of the Konkan (west Coast). It is situated about 47 kms. north of Mumbai, and is now known as Nalasopara.

In mid third century BC emperor Ashoka sent one of his missionaries Dhammarakshita, to Sopara to spread Buddhism in Western India. This edict is a testimony of this mission.

The script of the edict is Mauryan Brahmi.

Translation:

• King Devanampriyapriyadarsin (title of the king Ashoka) speaks thus.

• Men perform various ceremonies during illness, at the marriage of a son or a daughter, at the birth of a child (and) when setting out on a journey, on these and other such (occasions) men perform many ceremonies.

• But in such (cases) mothers and wives perform many and various trifling and useless ceremonies.

• Now, ceremonies should certainly be performed.

• But these (ceremonies) bear little fruit indeed.

• The following, however, bears much fruit indeed, viz the practice of morality.

• The following (are included), in this (viz) Proper courtesy to slaves and servants, reverence to elders, gentleness to animals, (and) liberality to Brahmanas and Shramanas; these and other such (virtues) are called the practice of morality.

• Therefore a father, or a son ....

These were the words of noble of Buddhism spreaded among the peoples of Soparaka (present Nalasopara) by the Buddhist sthaviras who were sent here in 3rd century BC in the reign of Maurya king Ashoka (Shown in IX Ashokan edict as above).

According to the Brahminical literature, in the Mahabharata, Soparaka was a holy place visited by Arjuna along with his other four brothers and performed worship in the shrines of Vasu, Ashvini, Vavaiswat, Aditya, Kuber, Indra,, Savitri, Vishnu, Bhava, Chandra, Divakara,, Varuna, Saraswati and Rudra etc nearby this place.

Sopara or Shurparaka finds mention in the Buddhist, Jain and Brahmin literature and all mentioned it an important wealthy city and emporium in Aparanta from third century BC. to fifteen century AD. About middle of 3rd century BC it flourished as a Buddhist centre with the effort of Mauryan king Ashoka who sent his missionary to this place to expand Buddhism.

In the Jain texts too, Soparaka had mentioned as one of the eighty four holy places of the Jainas. Of the eighty four Jain sects one is called surparaka or the sect originated in Sopara. Western India cave inscriptions contain six references on Sopara. These caves inscriptions are found in Karle, Nasik, Naneghat and Kanheri Caves. The most significant monument of this region is the Buddhist stupa or relic mound about one km west of Sopara town which is known as mound locally known as Burud Rajacha Kot.

From the assertion of Periplus that Sandanes controlled Bharukachcha- Sopara region. The scholars identified Sandane as kushana king Kanishka. In the 2nd century AD the son in law of Nahapana built cells, caves and water bodies for the

Buddhist monks at Varanas (Palanpur, Gujarat), Prabhasa, Bharukachcha, Dasapura, Goverdhana and Soparaga etc (Motichandra,1977;105).

When Gautama Buddha took nirvana and it is believed that in the same year Tambraparni (modern Sri Lanka) was attacked by a Prince of Lata (Gujarat) named Vijay Singh who went there via Soparaka by the sea route. Thereafter the name of modern Sri Lanka was placed "Singhala" after the last name "singh" of Vijaya Singh(Sakritayana:1952,35).

Another reference comes of Purna; a disciple of Gautama Buddha who was well-known for,"pre-eminent in preaching. "Purna is the shorter term of "Purnamaitreyaniputra" which means boundless preaching and compassion. Purna came from a rich and happy family of sunaparanta (sopara). He was very much loved by his parents. However, he felt that all the love and wealth in this world were temporary so he bid farewell to his relatives and took refuge in the Buddha. He vowed to spread the truth to salvage sentient beings. In view to spread the message of Buddhism in his native place he took permission from Buddha and came back to sunaparanta and taught dhamma to the peoples of Sunaparanta (Goenka,2010: 78).

One reference comes in the Tripitaka about Soparaka as; there was a poor person named Daruchiriya, who was the resident of Soparaka, heard the name of Buddha that one Sammyanka Buddha has taken birth and he was on movement to preach the noble to the people at Vaishali. He decided to meet Buddha and took departure from Soparaka to shravasti and then from there to Jetvan where he met to Buddha and gained blessing (Goenka,1995;37).

During the time of Gautama Buddha the expansion of Buddhism could not reach out of the country but it has deeply rooted beyond the area of Magadha and Rajgir upto the Himalayan, vindhyan, kurukshetra and koshi. After two months later of the nirvana of Gautama Buddha, first council was organized at Rajgir; a capital of Magadh by their main pupils to expand Buddhism. After one hundred years later, second council held at Vaishali to solve some contentious theme arose during that time in the sect. But when the third council were organized by Mogliputta Sthavira and he thought that measures should be taken to spread noble thoughts of the Buddhism among the people of outside country. In view of that he selected sthaviras for different region like Mahadeva sthavira to Mahinsak region, Rakshit sthavira to Vanvasi, Maharakshita sthavira to yonaka region (greek states), Maddhyama(Manjhim) sthavira to Himalayan states, Sonaka and Uttara sthavira to Swarna state, Mahendra along with Itthiya, Uttiya, Sambal and Bhatsal to Tambraparni (modern Srilanka). At the same point of time yonakadharama rakshita sthavira and Mahadharamarakshita sthavira were appointed and sent to Aparantha and Maharashtra respectively,

About middle of 3rd century BC it flourished as a Buddhist centre with the effort of Mauryan king Ashoka who sent his missionary to this place to expand Buddhism. The nomenclature of this place probably was after the name of Boddhisat Soparaka; former birth of Gautama Buddha. Soparaka Buddha himself is said to have visited this place and donated his nails and hairs to the devotee as a relic who erected stupa over them here (Gazetteer, 2006).

Western India cave inscriptions contain six references on Sopara. These caves inscriptions are found at Karle, Nasik, Naneghat and Kanheri. In the Silhara inscription now placed in the Chhatrapti Shivaji Vastu Sangrahalaya (Prince of Wales Museum) Mumbai, contain reference of Suparka and in one inscription of Saka Usavadatta it is stated as an important emporium of west India (Law,1954,299).

Nomenclature of Soparaka

The name of Sopara occurs in different accounts of the scholars as; Suryodgaman sutra mentioned as Supparaka, Mahavansho as supparakapattanam, legend of Purna as Surparaka, Yadavakosha as Surparaka, Mahabharata and srikantacharita as Surparaka, Sripalacharita, Jinaprabhasuri and at the Karle inscription it is mentioned as Soparaka, list of 84 gachchas as Sorparaka, Nasik inscription as Sorparaga, naneghat inscription as Soparaya, Ptolemy mentined as Supara, Priprlus as Ouppara, Kosmas as Sibor, Sihara copper plate as Surpparaka, Macudi as Subara, Ibn Haukal as Surabaya, Al Istakhari as Surbarah, Al Biruni and Al Idrisi as Subara, and Jordanus as Subera(Indraji,1882,273-328).

The nomenclature of this place probably was after the name of Boddhisat Suparak; former birth of Gautama Buddha. Soparaka himself is said to have visited this place and distributed his nails and hairs to a woman devotee as a relic who erected stupa in his reverence over it here(Reference of Tripitaka).

A vivid accounts are recorded in the jatakamala a collection of Buddhist story wherein reference occurred of Soparaka. In a story Aryasura gives a version of Soparaka who was a perfect and well versed in niryamaka sutra (Nautical science). Aryasura has conjectured that Sopara port was named after him (Motichandra,1977, 144-146). During the ancient time nautical science was quite developed. One who choose this line as a profession must be knowledgeable in different species in the sea, different coloures of the sea creatures, condition of the sea coasts, study of sea birds, marine rock etc. Beside that he should be awared of all seasons and climate (Motichandra,1977,144). Soparaka was well qualified in all these nautical knowledge because of his expertise he was famous and was demanded by the merchants even at his old age too. Once the merchants of swarnadvipa requested him to captain their ship but he refused by saying that he was quite old and would be unable to drive a ship but when persisted by the merchants he agreed to drive. After taking captainship of the ship they had a very rare experience in the sea voyage. Some saw changing colours of the sea and sky, different kind of sound and views of different creatures. Some passengers saw mermaids which appeared neither fish nor woman but Soparaka cleared their doubt by saying that those were fish of Khurmali sea. On the way Soparaka consoled the feared passengers and maintained his composure of mind when they reached at the end of earth hereafter travelled to the Dadhimala sea (Fuming sea), Agnimala sea (Red sea), Kushamala and Naamala (Motichandra,1977,145).

Tradition of making of Topes or Stupa

The tradition of making of topeor as stupa was even prior to Gautama Buddha's advent. From several passeges in the Pali Buddhistical annals, it revealed that topes or stupa dedicated to Krakuchanda, Kanaka and Kasyapa were in reversence prior to Gautama Buddha (Cunniagram, 1854:10).

As mention in Deerghanikaya, Mahaparinibbansutta that "Chatumahapathe tathagatasya thupo katabbo". "Tesam tam bhavisati deegharatam hitaya sukhaya". Tathagat ke astiavashesh ke sthapana ke liye bade chaurahon par stupe banana chahiye. Waha chirkal tak unke hita, sukha ke liye hoga. Means there should be a stupa erected over the relic of Tathagata (Buddha) on the centre where two road crossed each other, that would be for the welfare of him who made it for long time(Goenka, 1995, 66).

In the Mahavanso, the tradition of making of topes or stupa is clearly described which states that when any wealthy or powerful person was intended to built a tope in the name of Buddhistatva he used to erect first a pillar there recording his intentions thereafter pillar was removed when construction of tope begun.

In the foundation, the round stones were filled up and trodden down through elephant thereafter courses were raised one by one of fine clay, bricks, cement, kuruvinda stones, iron plates, divine incense (brought from Hemawanta, phalika stones (steatites), common stones, plates of brass (imbedded in kapittho gum which had been moisted with the milk of small red coco-nuts), and plates of silver(cemented vermilion mixed in oil of sesamum). The Plates of silver and brass and even of iron, were possibly small disc and course of phalika stone only a single slab; each deposited in the centre of the building (Cunningham;1854,169-78).

At the centre eight vases of gold and eight of silver were deposited and surrounded by eight gold and eight silver bricks again surrounded by one hundred and eight earthen vases. The brick layers were assembled for the masonry by beat of drums.

The placing of relic casket into the top was also associated with great religious ceremony. In the case of Duttagamini of cylone, on the evening of the day of full moon the king in a chariot drawn by four white horses carried the golden relic casket on his head surrounded by the canopy of dominion, towards the tope. The procession was headed an elephant whose name was Kandulo and who was a state elephant was fully decorated and dressed up and the chariot was followed by other elephants, horses and chariots. They were surrounded by people including men and women holding vases, baskets of flowers, torches and flags. The whole procession was performed with vocal and instrumental music in loud. On reaching to the tope king received relics from the chief sthavira and deposited them in the golden casket and offer bowing reverently and stood with raised hands and swearing afterward that "(he dedicate his kingdom to redeemer of the world the divine teacher, the bearer of the three canopy; the canopy of heavenly host, the canopy of mortals and the canopy of eternal emancipation)". King mounting eastern sides descends in to the relic chamber and deposited relic casket and thereafter relic chamber was closed. After enshrining the relics, the dome was closed and provided by a square capital. Thereafter the work plastering and installation of canopies were carried out.

Alexander Cunningham in his 'the Bhilsa Topes' has very clearly defined stupa into three distinct kinds viz. Dedicatory, Funereal and Memorial. The Dedicatory stupa is one dedicated to Supreme Buddha or Adi Buddha. The largest topes such as those of Sanchi, Satdhara, and Bhojpur in district Vidisha in Madhya Pradesh are placed by him under this category. The Adi Buddha is invisible being who pervaded all space, no deposit was made, but the light was suppose to occupy the interior and was typified on the outside by a pair of eyes placed on each of the four sides either of the base or the crown of the edifice(chaitya).The Funeral stupa are those where ashes of the dead were found. These are found numerous as they were built of all sizes and of all kind of material. The Memorial stupa are those which are built upon a celebrated place.

In the Tibetan Buddhism the stupa dedicated to Celestial Buddha are called Chhod-ten while the stupa dedicated to mortal Buddha are called Dung-ten (Cunningham:1854, 9,171,173).

3

Background of Stupa Excavation at Nalasopara

W.W. Loch noticed this mound in Nalasopara which was locally called as Burud Rajacha killa (Fortress of Burud king) that is, The Bamboo making king's fort, was too small for a fort and was shaped like a Buddhist burial mound.In the christmas last in the month of February James Campbell went with Mr. Pandit Bhagwanlal Indraji, the well-known scholar and antiquarian to Nalasopara and with Mr. Mullock the collector to Nalasopara and examined the fort (then fort is referred for the mound). Bhagwan Lal was satisfied that it was a Buddhist tope or relic mound, and that it had not been opened. We accordingly arranged, with Mr. Mullock's help, to open it during the Easter holidays. Under Bhagwan Lal's guidance four gangs of men were set to work, two at the east and west end of the base of the mound and two at the east and west ends of the domed top. A passage was cut through the mound about four feet broad, rising towards the centre, above twelve feet below the top of the dome, the bricks were found to be built in the form of a small chamber about two feet nine inches squares" (Indraji: 284-285). In view to bring that excavation into the notice of then government Campbell wrote a letter to the Collector on 29 April 1882 stating;"I have the honour to forward for submission to government, an account of the relics found in sopara tope near Bassein which was opened between 7th-to 10th April 1882 under the guidance of Mr. Bhagwan Lal Indraji. I should be obliged if you would bring it to the notice of the government the service of Pandit Bhagwan Lal Indraji, without whose skilful Superintendence the work could not have been carried out"(Indraji: 1882;285).

Bhagwanlal Indaraji

Bhagwanlal Indaraji (1839-88) came in the horizon of archaeology in 1861 when the foundation of the Archaeological Survey of India was instituted. During that time scholars like Charles Wilkins, B. G. Babington, John Wilson, James Prinsep, Alexender Cunningham, B. H. Hodgson, Edward Norris, George Buehler, John F. Fleet, James Furgusson, James Burgess, Edward Thomas, Walter Elliot, J.F. Fleet, William Erskine, W.H. Sykes, W. H. Wathen, James Bird, John Stevenson, Col. Tod, James cambel, A. K. Forbs, and among the India scholars R. L. Mitra, Dr. Bhaudaji Lad, Prof. Jambhekar, were working in the field of archaeology and its allied disciplines (Virchand:2012:16-39).

Since born in historical place Junagad he made his first attempt at his native place to decipher the Rudradaman inscription at Girnar thus appeared as an epigraphist. Thereafter he deciphered three most important inscriptions of Indian history- those of Ashoka, Rudradaman, and Skandagupta. In 1861 A.K. Forbes recommended his name to Dr. Bhaudaji Lad of Bombay. With the association of Bhaudaji Lad, Bhagwan Lal visited most parts of the country for archaeological exploration and documentation and visited Ajanta, Pitalkhora, Elephanta, Kanheri, Nasik, Karla, Bhaja, Bedsa, Junner, Ellora, and Naneghat during 1862. During 1865 and 1874 he toured

Sanchi, Sonari, Udaigiri, Eran, Mandu, Delhi, Mathura, bairat, Kalsi, Benaras, Sarnath, Allahabad, Gadwa, Kushinagar, Lauriyanandangarh, bodhgaya, Bihar, Oddisa caves, Puri, Ganjam, Warangal, Kolahpur, Kashmir, Taxila, Peshawar, Yusufzai (in Baluchstan) and Nepal and collected data in the form of photography, transcript and field notes. After the touring of vast area of Indian sub continent Bhagwanlal Indraji emerged as a true archaeologist of multidisciplinary approach.

During 1867-68 Bhagwanlal Indraji undertook a small excavation in Junagarh closed to river Sonerekha and yielded few sculptures. After the disassociation from Burgess, he enjoyed great reputation and found the opportunity to make important contribution in the archaeology in the gazetteer. The archaeological skill of Bhagawanlal Indraji was very much known to James Campbell beside that he may have heard the high regard of James Gibbs for Bhagawanlal. James Gibbs was the same person who recommended his name and passed the motion for inclusion of Bhagawanlal in the Bombay Branch Royal Asiatic Society as a Honorary member (Virchand: 2012;154- 209).

There occurred three important incidents in the life of Bhagwanlal Indraji which brought him in the sphere of Indian archaeology. One was his birth in the historical place where he could had childhood attachment with art and heritage of Junagarh, second, his association with Dr. Bhaudaji Lad in 1861 who gave him opportunity to elaborate his archaeological skill through touring of the most parts of the country, and third when detached his association from Burges and started work independently with James Campbell for gazetteer of the Bombay Presidency in 1880. He was the first who read kharvela and Satakarni inscriptions. He identified kharvela king of Kalinga and Naneghat inscription of Satakarni. He also proved existence of Traikutaka, identified Vakatakas and restored konkan Mauryas and Rashhtrakutas to their rightful place in history (Virchand:2012;58- 63).

Earlier Evidence from the Site

The account of Nalasopara described by Bhagwanlal Indraji revealed that the present mound was once a fort of Burud king who lived a very simple life with his queen over here with their occupation of basket making. Therefore he was called Burud king. On the basis of information locally gathered by Bhagwanlal Indraji says that the mound was also a residence of a pathan fakir named Shaikh Amir, who had the knowledge of alchemy and magic and because of that he received respect among the local residents. But basically he was a plunder who employed four persons to rob for him at night for which he dug six feet deep pit inside the mound to keep the stolen property. Later on he was caught with stolen property. Thereafter this mound was occupied by Ramjan Khan who was his disciple and his grave was dug near the mound (Indraji: 1882;293-94.).

The excavation was carried out here by Bhagwanlal Indraji in three days from 7th April to 9th April 1882. In three days, mound was dug, from the centre top in east-west, upto basement and a square brick chamber measuring .90 x .90 mts was found below the base level of stupa. The chamber was pyramidal in shape on the top and filled up with circular stone coffer inside. In fact yielded good results and incredible antiquities recovered in the form of stupa, eight metal images ; Maitreya and seven manushi Buddha in metal casket, pieces of earthern ware, a silver coin of Gautmiputra Shatkarni and golden flowers etc. Beside that 8th rock edicts were recovered from Sopara by Bhagwanlal Indraji which was found in fragments.

In the 1939-40 excavation was carried out by M.M. Qureshi of the Archaeological Survey of India yielded remarkable structural evidences including miniature stupas. He exposed two stupas at the south side of main stupa and several other votive stupa and round structures. Beside that six feet wide circumambulatory path were exposed. Among the antiquity, glazed pottery of later period, coins of Satavahana period, Gadhya coins of 8th-12th century and coins of Muslim rulers were also yielded from here but unfortunately no report on the excavation were traced out. However some of the photographs of the excavation, structures and antiquities are available in the Mumbai and Aurangabad circles for references.

Other sculptures found from the Nalasopara are stone images of Brahma, Surya, Mahishasurmardini, Varah lifting Prithvi, Gauri-Shankar, dancing Shiva, and Surasundari with a parrot dating from 11th to 14 century AD, and Ambika and memorial stones of late medieval period.

In 1956 N. A. Gore, Librarian of Asiatic Society of Bombay discovered 9th Ashokan rock edict which is now placed in the Chhatrapati Shivaji Maharaj Vastu Sangrahalaya(old name Prince of wales Museum) Mumbai.

In 1981, 19 bronze pieces of 14th century were found accidently from Nalasopara.

Excavation of Mound by Bhagwanlal Indraji

The mound consisting of the main stupa was a large dome surrounded by the rectangular ruined rubble wall. Its height was 9.30 m and diameter 20.10 m. It was surrounded with bushes, jack mango and coconut trees planted by a pathan fakir Shaikh Amir when he occupied this place for his residence.

The excavation was carried out in three days from 7th April to 9th April 1882. In three days mound was dug, from the centre top in east-west, upto basement. The first day digging was done upto 2.40 m (8 feets) which yielded pair of scissors, a two and coin of 1841, shivari paice, fragment of glass bottles, porcelain and bones of sheep within depth of 1.80 m. All of these traces were of Shaikh Amirs plunder. In the second day digging reached in the depth of 1.20m (4 feets) without having any yields. On the third day a square brick chamber measuring .90 x .90 m was found below the base level of stupa. The chamber was pyramidal in shape on the top and filled up with circular stone coffer inside.

Mound Locally known as Barud Rajacha Kot

The site under discussion (lat. 19° 24' 51.74" N, log. 72° 47' 41.47" E) possesses an area of 2.57 acres under protection which includes a large stupa and other votive stupas within the premise. Being a potential archaeological site it was protected by the name of mound locally known as Barud King by the Archaeological Survey of India as a monument of national importance F-18-22/37 – F, dated 25.03.1938.

4

Conservation of Site

In 2011-12 a scientific clearance work was undertaken by the Archaeological Survey of India under Mumbai Circle at the site under special work. This site was earlier excavated twice; in 1882 and in 1939-40, so there was no question of systematic excavation to be carried out again but, since whole the site had developed exclusively with earth and vegetation growth due to not attend of restoration work for long time so it was inevitably required to first clear those debris and vegetation and expose underneath structures before restoration.

The site premise comprised total 2.57 acres of land which was not properly protected by the boundary wall. Although there was the remains of old fencing over there provided with wire mesh and concrete pillars of which pillars were removed off and the site was open to access from all sides. Since it locates in the village therefore it was prone to the access of the cattles of the villagers too. Within the site the structures includes a main brick stupa and heaps of small structures around the main brick stupa. The brick stupa was open with growth of small vegetation over it and dense vegetation around them. Beside that large trees of palm surrounded the whole premise. The heaps of small structures around were so covered with debris and vegetation that one could not identified them whether they were in fact a heap of undulating land or structure lying underneath. During the time of Bhagwanlal Indraji an excavation was carried out here but that was completely an unsystematic as there was no excavation method evolved till that point of time. The systematic excavation had evolved during the time of Sir Mortimer wheeler some times in 1944. After exposing of antiquities and sculptures from the excavation the mound had left to the mercy of god without care and maintenance. The site was not properly protected from 1968 to 1939-40 till the second excavation was carried out by M.M. Qureshi and it remained without any care and maintenance. The brick stupa within the site which was excavated in 1882 by Bhagwanlal Indraji measures 84.97m in circumference, 27.05m in dia and 6.00m in height from ground level and having remains of steps at eastern side was in extant. Although measurments of the tope described by him are different from the measurement taken by the author. The dome of it was badly destroyed at the middle portion as it was used for the pathway by the local peasants and because of that stupa had divided into two parts having a large gap between the central and corner sides. The outer course of the brick masonry of the dome all around had completely removed and because of that the inner masonry was fallen and damaged at different places and in different depth. The only preserved part of the structure was medhi which was buried into the earth and few courses of it had merely visible.

At the first stage of conservation work we had to go up to drum level so that to find its condition whether its wall were straight or out of plumb because at different sides at the exterior, it had been covered with earth of diverse deposits somewhere it was higher and somewhere lower. Simultaneously brick layer of the visible medhi did not appear in straight position. So we were of the opinion that structure had tilted towards southward.

For this a detailed drawings including plan and elevation were prepared.

In the meantime the surrounding area of the main strupa was cleared from the vegetation. Of them large tree of palm could not be cleared because small stupas and other miniature structures buried underneath were in the clutch of their roots so their removal took place gradually after clearing debris and cutting roots one by one. This clearance of work started from east–south end to south.

As mentioned earlier that land was undulating due to structures buried underneath, after clearance of vegetation the remains of top surface of the structure were exposed. These were the same structures exposed in the excavation of 1939-40 carried out by M.M. Quraishi and which could not be restored after excavation that time and after gap of long time they went again underneath and covered with debris. After seeing upper most layers of the votive stupas we inferenced their depth upto two to three courses but in fact when clearance work went on the exposed structures were found of five to twelve courses in square, rectangular and circular shapes. They all were votive stupas built for commemorative purpose around the main stupa as we generally found in Nalanda, Vaishali, Vikramshila and other similar site in Bihar and other parts of the country. These structures are built of burnt bricks measuring 40 x 23 x 8 cms, 40 x 25 x 8 cms, 30 x 23 x 8 cms, and 25 x 25 x .025 cms, and located to each other in divers distance from 25 cms to 7 m. Although there is no certain alignment determined for erecting them but they are built in such a pattern that one can easily sit near for worship and make circumambulation around these stupas after main stupa.

One by one each votive stupa were exposed, documented and dismantled and thereafter reset on the leveled foundation, consolidated with traditional mortar (Lime mixed with mud). During opening of these structures it was found that earlier they were simply laid directly on the levelled earth and due to that all the structures are found tilted and architectural members dislocated from its original place. Therefore decision of providing foundation was taken up.

The stupas were fallen at the centre and at the surrounding sides but before taking work, the upper most level of outer brick course were identified and documented so that to initiate repair upto that level with matching masonry and mortar originally used therein. The filling of the stupa was not a usual filling, rather it was with a specific arrangement of bricks that

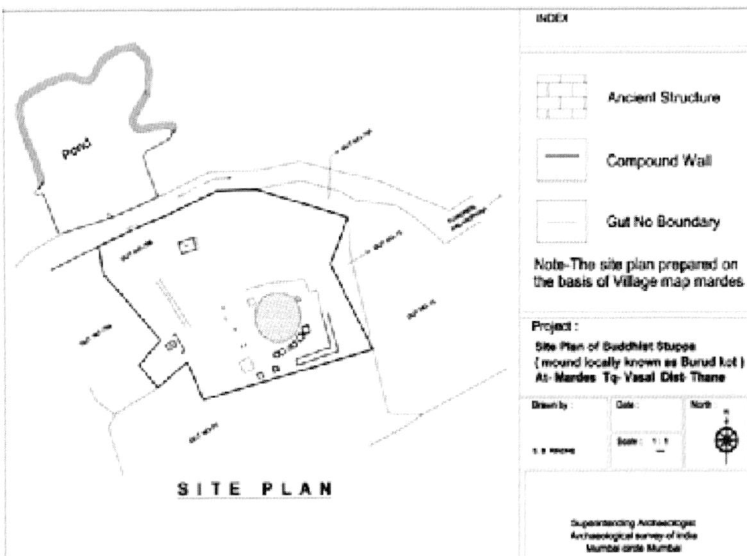

Fig. 3. Site plan of Mound locally known as Burud Kot, Nalasopara.

were maintained as per its original. Bricks were arranged one above the other by leaving half space lower brick binding in traditions mortar. These all were of clear plan and elevation except some layers missing at the top. Each was restored upto original foundation level without adding new bricks. The mortar used therein was made of mud mortar and same were used in masonry.

Beside that more area has been chosen for clearance which probably had not taken earlier for excavation by M.M. Qureshi and no stratigraphical study has been done. The structures, pottery sherds, and other antiquities recovered from here were documented.

STRUCTURAL DETAILS

MAIN STUPA : 1

Diameter of main stupa	:	27.05 m
Circumference	:	84.97 m
Height of stupa from existing ground level	:	6.00 m
Average plot area under possesion	:	10407.25 sqm (112023.64 Sqf)

Pl. 1. Main stupa, Mound Locally known as Burud king, Nalasopara.

Scientific Clearance Carried Out

During the course of scientific clearance votive stupas around the main stupa were exposed one by one followed by their restoration. More than eleven votive stupas of square and circular shapes are exposed, from the east-south side and accordingly numbering of each votive stupa has been made starting from stupa No. 2 of the east-south side to south in clockwise direction upto stupa No.11, the details of which are as under;

VOTIVE STUPA : 2

Side	:	**South-East side, Square**
Shape	:	Square
Height	:	.90 m
Dimension	:	Top3.90x3.60, m
Basement	:	4.30x 4.30 m
Distance from main stupa	:	1.80m
Distance between 2 and 3	:	0.20 m

Pl.2. Votive stupa at Mound Locally known as Burud king, Nalasopara.

At the South-east corner of the main stupa has exposed a stupa of .90m height. It is almost square in shape and the masonry of bricks goes from below to top in decreasing trend measuring 4.30x4.30 m at the basement and 3.90 x 3.60 m at the top. A simple molding on each side of wall has done in such a way that it corresponds with simple vedibandha moldings of a nagar temple. Each side of the wall has hollow moldings done at two points having the gap of 1.18 m to each other. At the lower part, the bricks are arranged straight towards upside upto 4 courses thereafter courses goes in pyramidical trend up to 5 courses. The upper surface was of uneven level with different size of bricks.

VOTIVE STUPA : 3

Side	:	**South-East side of main stupa**
Shape	:	Circular
Height	:	.90 m
Dimension: dia	:	3.50m
Distance from main stupa	:	.90m
Distance between B to C	:	.2.0 m

Pl. 3. Votive stupa at Mound Locally known as Burud king, Nalasopara.

Just west side of the stupa 2 and at the south-east of the main stupa has this circular stupa exposed. Only two courses are visible before the expose, when cleared upto its functional level the layer of ten courses has been yielded with its architectural members dislodged from its western side. This structure was raised on a bed of brick bats broken in small pieces and trodden with clay. Measuring 3.50 m in dia, its courses are arranged in slight decreased trends towards upside. Devoid of any ornamentation it is simply raised with fine mud mortar between the bricks.

VOTIVE STUPA : 4

Side	:	**South-East side**
Shape	:	Circular
Height	:	.90 m
Dimension: dia	:	3m
Distance from main stupa	:	2.60m
Distance between 1 to 2	:	0.20m
4 to 5	:	0.60 mts

Pl. 4. Votive stupa at Mound Locally known as Burud king, Nalasopara.

Just west to the Stupa 3 at a distance of only 0.20 m has this stupa recovered. It has 3.00 m dia and a height of .90 m from the ground level. The brick masonry is done in a flemish pattern which goes up in decreasing pattern. One course has provided at the foundation wherein two another course are laid down straight thereafter masonry decreases half to one inch towards upside.

VOTIVE STUPA : 5

Side	:	West side of main stupa
Shape	:	Square
Height	:	.60 m
dimension		
top	:	2.10x 2.10 mts.
Basement	:	2.55x 2.55 m
Distance from main stupa	:	3.20m.
Distance between 4 to5	:	0.60 m 5 to 6 2.10m

Pl. 5. Votive stupa at Mound Locally known as Burud king, Nalasopara.

This stupa exists at the west of main stupa. Having square on plan it measures 2.55 x 2.55 m at its lower part and 2.10 x

2.10m at the top. Originally, this stupa was of ten courses but upper two are missing. The brick masonry of this stupa has done in a step pattern. One course has laid down for foundation over which rests three straight courses. This is further surmounted with four straight courses. The brick masonry is done in flemish pattern.

VOTIVE STUPA : 6

Side	:	South-west
Shape	:	circular
Height	:	.80 m
Distance: dia	:	3.10 m
Distance from main stupa	:	4.10m
Distance between 5 to 6	:	2.10m
Distance between 6 to 7	:	.50 m

Pl. 6. Votive stupa at Mound Locally known as Burud king, Nalasopara.

This stupa is exposed at the south of main stupa and South-west of stupa 5 at a distance of 4.10 m and 2.10 m respectively. It consists of ten courses upto a height of 0.80 m from the ground level. This stupa, like others, is devoid of any ornamentation but design wise it can be easily differentiate to the stupas as discussed above. At the basement one course is laid down over which the brick course raises in inward trend upto 4 courses thereafter another two raises outward. Over these outward courses surmounts three another courses again in inward pattern. This sort of masonry arrangement of the stupa reflects a pot like design of the structure.

VOTIVE STUPA : 7

Side	:	South-west
Shape	:	circular
Height	:	1.00 m
dimension: Dia	:	3.10 m
Distance from main stupa	:	5.80m
Distance between 6 to 7	:	.50 m
Distance between 7 to 8	:	3.80m

Pl. 7. Votive stupa at Mound Locally known as Burud king, Nalasopara.

An another circular stupa is exposed at the south-west of main stupa and west of stupa 6 at a distance of 5.80 m and 0.50 m respectively. It consists of twelve courses with a height of 1.00 m. Whole structure rests on a single course basement. Over which has five sets of courses consisting in 2 +1+2+2+4 sets arranged in outward- inward alteration except top most set of four courses which raised in decreasing trend towards upside.

VOTIVE STUPA : 8

Side	:	South-west
Shape	:	Square
Height	:	1.10 m
Dimension	:	Top 2.50 x 2.50
basement	:	3.70 x 3.70 m
Distance from main stupa	:	13.40 m
Distance between 7 to 8	:	3.80 m
Distance between 8 to 9	:	6.90m

Pl. 8. Votive stupa at Mound Locally known as Burud king, Nalasopara.

This stupa has exposed to the south-west corner of the main stupa and to the east of stupa 9 at a distance of 13.40 m and 6.90 m respectively. It is closer to stupa 7 at a distance of 3.80m. Square on plan, it measures 3.70 x 3.70 m at the basement and 2.50 x 2.50 m at the top. Originally it was made of more than 12 courses over a single layered basement. The masonry work of this stupa has done square within the square pattern. Over the basement, one set of six courses of bricks are arranged in vertical strait, thereafter leaving space inward, another set over it of more than seven courses are arranged.

VOTIVE STUPA : 9

Side	:	South-west
Shape	:	Square
Height	:	.70 m from ground level
Dimension	:	Top 2.70 x 2.70,
basement	:	3.40 x 2.70 m.
Distance from main stupa	:	17.90 m.
Distance between stupa 7 to 8	:	3.80 m
Distance between stupa 8 to 9	:	6.90 m

Pl. 9. Votive stupa at Mound Locally known as Burud king, Nalasopara.

This stupa is exposed at the south-west corner of the main stupa at a distance of 17.90 m.Prior to expose of this stupa, surface was plain and there was no indication of structure. But as debris had cleared, a stupa of almost square shape and 0.70 m of height appeared. It has six courses of brick masonry having upper one consisting of four courses and lower with two measuring 2.60 x 2.80 m dimension. At north face between lower and upper course there is a mud filling of 0.20 m.

South-east corner of the stupa has badly damaged and bricks missing. Whole the structure is disturbed on its plan exclusively towards south-west corner.

Around the foundation of the structure are brick bats, boulders provided with earth to give outer support to the stupa. It goes more than 0.30 m all around the structure.

VOTIVE STUPA : 10

Side	:	South-west
Shape	:	Square
Height	:	.75 m from ground level.
Dimension	:	6.90 x 6.90 m
Distance from main stupa	:	14 m
Distance between stupa 9 to 10	:	3.30m
Brick size	:	8 x.25x .40m

Pl. 10. Votive stupa at Mound Locally known as Burud king, Nalasopara.

At the south-west corner of the main stupa has a stupa found in very decrepit condition at its top and south-west side. This is larger than the other found miniature stupas within the premise. Square in shape, it measures 6.90 x 6.90 m with 0.75 m of height. This stupa was buried inside with earth, rubbles and a ruined dressed stone wall which might had exposed during the excavation carried out in 1882 by Bhagwanlal Indraji and thereafter by M.M. Qureshi in 1939-40. Before expose of this structure it was presumed that a rubble platform would come in north-south direction but as the debris had cleared a surface of the brick appeared underneath. The foundation is provided with brickbats combined with fine earth which goes 0.60 m in depth. This brickbats combined with mortar with fine earth is also provided 1.2 m to all around of the stupa to give support to it.

The interesting thing about this stupa is that it is like stupa 9, sunk and disturbed at the south west corner. All the courses were missing at this corner.

VOTIVE STUPA : 11

Side	:	North side
Shape	:	Square
Measurement	:	0.25x0.25x0.025 m.

Pl. 11. Votive stupa at Mound Locally known as Burud king, Nalasopara.

A square brick structure has been exposed at the north corner of main stupa. This structure has laid in north-south direction measuring 0.25 x 0.25 x 0.025m. The remarkable things about this structure is that it has composed of fine small square burnt bricks. Consisting of about 12 courses it has covered with a thick deposit of 0.70 m earth thereafter by an another brick layer of two courses. Such a gap between the two certainly shows two different cultural periods, the former one contemporary to the main stupa while the later to the other votive stupas found around the main stupa.

Other structures found at North-West Corner

Before taking the clearance work from south-west to west-north we had a presumption of finding miniature stupas of almost the same dimension and pattern as found at south-west corner of the main stupa but as proceeded towards north about 6 mts from stupa 10 the remains of wall were exposed. On the top surface of which there was an elevated alignment of around 90 mts in length which we thought an accumulation occurred during earlier excavation but in fact that was the foundation of rubble wall of late period probably built during the time of Raja Burud about which Bhagawanlal Indraji had briefly accounted. This foundation of wall has found made in imperfect masonry, probably using huge well dressed stone of main stupa when he took this place for his dwell.

Therefore the corner of the foundation has laid down with those dressed stones and middle part of it filled up with undressed rubbles of varying size and loose earth. This foundation of the wall runs upto 90 m without its continuity from south-west to west-north side so it is obvious that during the time of excavation carried out by Bhagawnlal Indraji this portion of wall was not exposed and the reason of discontinuation seems vandalism occurred after leaving this place by Raja Burud.

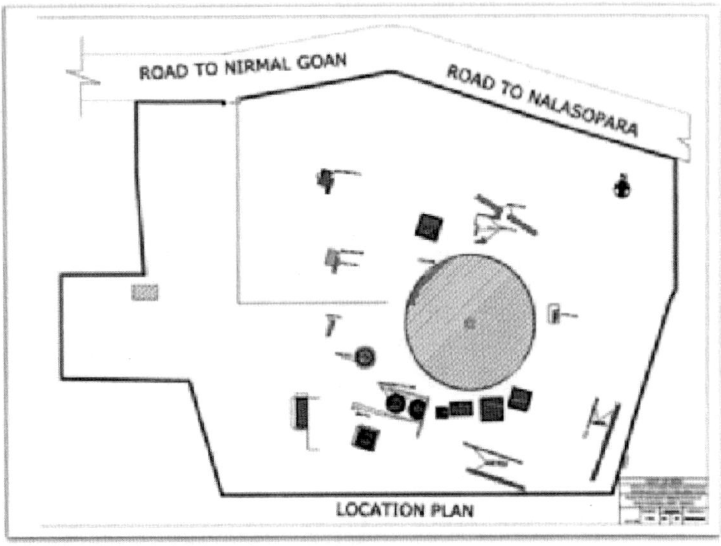

Fig. 4. Showing main stupa and other votive stupas.

About 2.10 m deep of the foundation of this rubble wall has two brick structure found at a quite distance from the wall towards north-east side. Of them one is a two coursed brick platform and other square votive stupa 11. The brick platform is oblong and laid in north-south direction measuring 3 x 1 m. As the clearance diverted towards east side an another platform of 1 x 1 m with three coursed were exposed between the platform and stupa 11 which indicate that this is an integral part of the platform, however, they both forms a gap of 230 m to each other.

Stone Votive Stupa

A stone votive stupa has been found at the south-west side of the main stupa. Alike in cylindrical design it has a Buddha image carved on the bottom. Buddha is shown in padmasana mudra having its left hand resting on the right feet crossed onto jangha and right hand touching right leg. A much worn out image has shown in a semi round arched niche. On the top of the stupa has eight perpendicular lines shown arose from a centre point which probably indicates eight cardinal directions.

Inscription

The abundance of inscription in the Buddhist sites are very common but during scientific clearance over here no such inscription was found that reveals more information about the site. At the eastern side of the main stupa there is an evidence of rubble wall as stated above, that surrounds the main stupa. Although it is badly damaged and it is not possible to determine its exact width and length but in spite of that the alignment of the wall can be determined on the basis of base course running from north-south direction. Towards the south-east side there is a stone slab of about 1.5 m dimension bearing alphabets of 6 nos . On the upper side has four alphabets out of it two (left side alphabets) are completely wiped out while right side two appears "sa" and "bha" however the lower right appears "ka".

OTHER ANTIQUITIES

Beside that numbers of fragment of architectural members of stone was obtained from here which are of worth description. These includes lamp, grinder, fragment of vedibanda part of temple, cap stone and other parts of railings, votive stupa, base of pillar and pottery of historical period. The found of some temple fragments over here indicates the existence of temple nearby this site which at present is not in extant. Beside that interesting thing about the architectural members are finding of members of vedika which generally raised around the stupa. We have numbers of the stupa sites where vedika or railings had been found around the stupa. Out of them, vedikas of Sanchi, Bharhut and Bodhgaya are exclusively decorated. At Sopara fragments of vedika found are very least in number (3-4 fragments) and they all are plain and devoid of any ornamentation. The fragment include base of pillar, cap stone (Ushanish) and pillar (Thaba). All the architectural members are at the site. The details of these antiquities are as under;

1.	**Object**	:	Stone Lamp (Pl. 12)
	Material	:	Stone
	Size	:	Length : 7.5cm
			Height : 5.7cm
	Description	:	A stone lamp found from the stupa no 3.

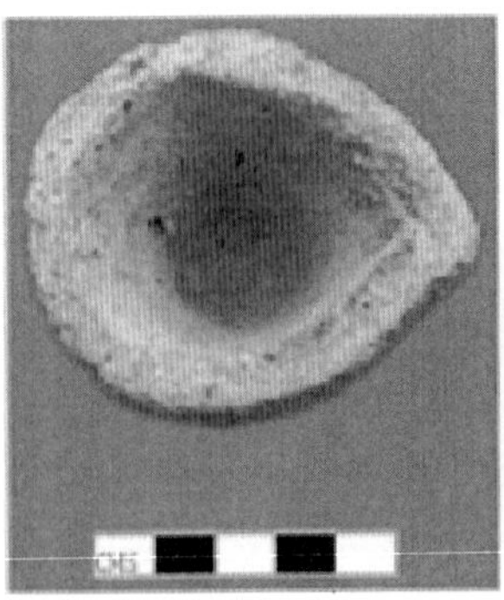

2. **Object** : Grinder (Pl. 13)
   Material : Stone
   Diameter : 7.0cm
   Length : 10.2cm
   Description : A fragment of stone grinder is found from south-west corner of the main stupa.

3. **Object** : Broken part of sharpner. (Pl. 14)
   Material : Stone
   Size : Length : 9.0cm
   Width : 5.0cm
   Description : A part of sharpner is found near stupa no 4.

4. **Object** : Broken fragments of temple. (Pl. 15)

Material : Stone

Size : Length : 40.0cm Width : 38.0cm
Height : 60.0cm

Description : The fragments of temple are found from the south-west corner of the main stupa. These are parts of vedibandha.

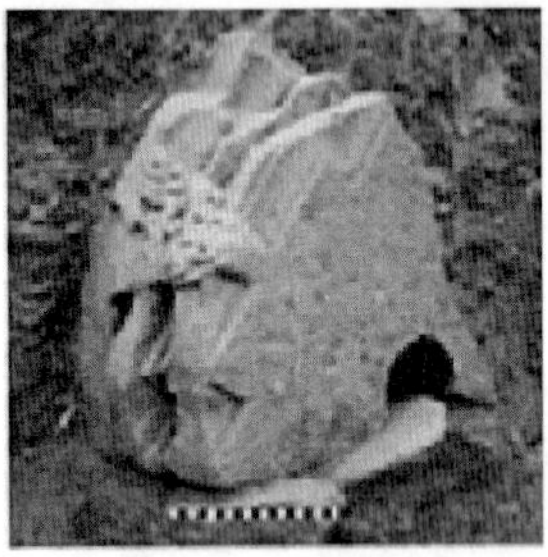

5. **Object** : Fragment of the walls of temple. (Pl. 16)

Material : Stone

Size : Length : 94.0cm
Width : 36.0cm
Height : 25.0cm

Description : An another fragment of the walls of the temple is found from the south-west corner of the main stupa.

6.	**Object**	:	Votive stupa. (Pl. 17)
	Material	:	Stone
	Size	:	Diameter : 38.0cm Height : 89.0cm
	Description	:	Found at the south-west side of the main stupa. Alike in cylindrical **Size** it has a Buddha image in padmasanamudra carved on the bottom within a niche. On the top of the stupa has eight perpendicular lines shown arose from a centre point which probably indicates eight cardinal directions.

7.	**Object**	:	Votive stupa. (Pl. 18)
	Material	:	Stone
	Size	:	Length : 0.90 m Width : 0.50 m Height : 0.25 m
	Description	:	Unidentified fragment.

8.	**Object**	:	Fragment of railing. (Pl. 19)
	Material	:	Stone
	Size	:	Length : 1.70 m Width : 0.40 m Height : 0.30 m
	Description	:	A fragment of railing is found from the south side of the main stupa.

9.	**Object**	:	Fragment of railing. (Pl. 20)
	Material	:	Stone
	Size	:	Length : 1.20 m Width : 0.40 m Height : 0.30 m
	Description	:	A fragment of vedika is found, from the south side of the main stupa.

10.	**Object**	:	Fragment of temple wall. (Pl. 21)
	Material	:	Stone
	Size	:	Length : 1.10 m Width : 0.30 m Height : 0.20 m
	Description	:	A fragment of the walls of the temple is found from the south-west corner of the main stupa.

11.	**Object**	:	Fragment of railing. (Pl. 22)
	Material	:	Stone
	Size	:	Length : 1.55 m Width : 0.40 m Height : 0.30 m
	Description	:	This fragment of stone appears thaba of the vedika of stupa.

12.	**Object**	:	Stone fragment. (Pl.23)
	Material	:	Stone
	Size	:	Length : 1.20 m Width : 0.40 m Height : 0.30 m
	Description	:	Unidentified fragment.

13. **Object** : Temple fragment. (Pl. 24)
Material : Stone
Size : Length : 0.80 m
Width : 0.40 m
Height : 0.15 m
Description : A fragment of temple with having grooves for fitting clamps.

14. **Object** : Unidentified stone fragment. (Pl. 25)
Material : Stone
Size : Length : 1.00 m
Width : 0.30 m
Height : 0.60 m
Description : Unidentified fragment.

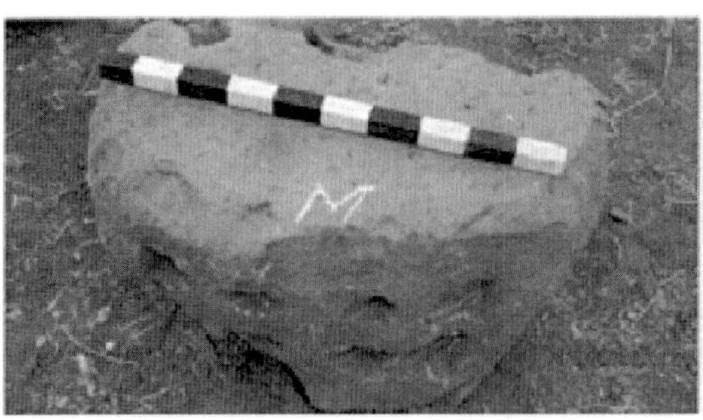

15. **Object** : Fragment of railing. (Pl. 26.)
Material : Stone
Size : Length : 35.0cm
Width : 33.0cm
Height : 20.0cm
Description : A base for fixing thaba is found from the west side of the main stupa.

16. **Object** : Fragment of Ushanisha. (Pl. 27.)
Material : Stone
Size : Length : 70.0cm Width : 40.0cm
Height : 20.0cm
Description : A fragment of ushanisha of vedika is found from the south-west side of the main stupa.

17. **Object** : Unidentified stone fragment. (Pl. 28)
Material : Stone
Size : Length : 30.0cm
Width : 30.0cm
Height : 35.0cm
Description : Unidentified fragment.

18. **Object** : Ushanisha; a part of railing. (Pl. 29)
Material : Stone
Size : Length : 70.0cm
Width : 40.0cm
Height : 40.0cm
Description : Ushanisha of railing found from the west side of the main stupa.

19.	**Object**	:	Broken part of pillar of railing. (Pl. 30)
	Material	:	Stone
	Size	:	Length : 55.0cm Width : 55.0cm Height : 25.0cm
	Description	:	A broken part of pillar.

20.	**Object**	:	Broken part of pillar of railing. (Pl.31)
	Material	:	Stone
	Description	:	A pillar with the grooves for fitting clamps.

21. **Object** : A broken part of pillar with grooves. (Pl. 32)

Material : Stone

Description : A pillar with the grooves for fitting clamps.

22. **Object** : A broken part of pillar base with groove. (Pl. 33)

Material : Stone

Description : A pillar base of the vedika with mark of groove found from the west side of the main stupa.

23. **Object** : A fragment of temple. (Pl. 34)
Material : Stone
Description : A temple fragment found from the south-west side of the main stupa.

24. **Object** : A fragment of temple. (Pl. 35)
Material : Stone
Description : A temple fragment found from the south-west side of the main stupa.

25. **Object** : A fragment of temple wall. (Pl.36)
Material : Stone
Description : A basefragment of pillar of vedika with grooves.

26. **Object** : A fragment of temple wall. (Pl.37)
Material : Stone
Description : A fragment of wall (Obverse).

27. **Object** : A fragment of temple wall. (Pl. 38)

Material : Stone

Description : A fragment of wall of the temple is found from the north side of the main stupa.

28. **Object** : A fragment of temple wall. (Pl. 39)

Material : Stone

Description : A fragment of wall with grooves for fitting clamps.

POTTERY

Early historical pottery including red ware and glazed pottery has been found from here during scientific clearance work. Among the sherds they include parts of rim of globular pot, sherds of dish, sherds of rim of carinated handi. The details of which are described as under;

Three sherds of early historic period are found from the south side of the main stupa. The lavigated clay, well fixed and manufactured in the fast wheel are the main characteristics of the pottery. The details are described as below;

I. Fragment of a globular pot with high neck and outgoing rounded undercut rim, decoration of incised line in the form of long oblique strokes on the junction of shoulder of the body.

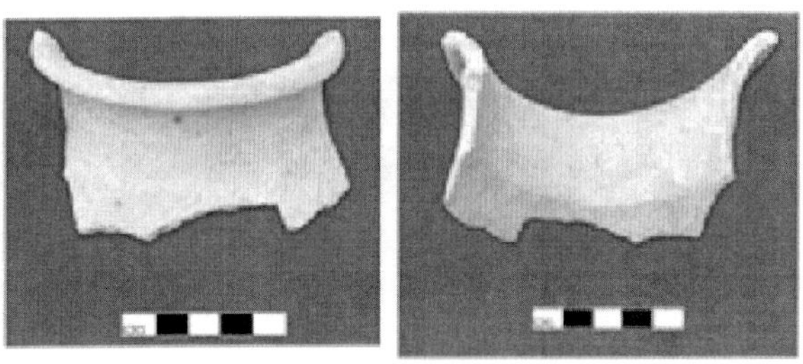

Pl. 40. Early historical pottery sherds.

II. Probably a part of dish which has rounded rim. This dish has attached on stand, the adjustment of attaching stand is made on the base.

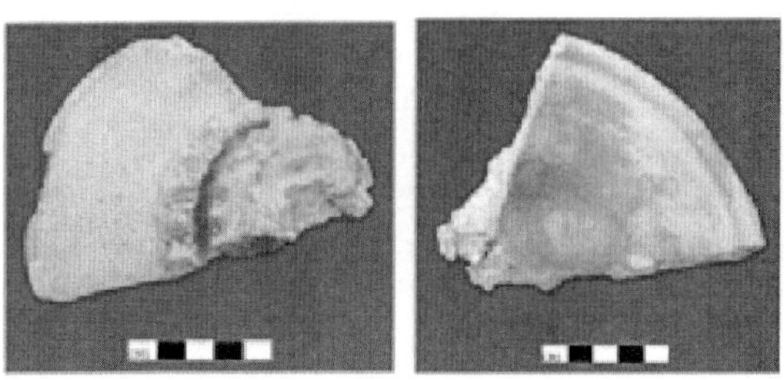

Pl. 41. Sherds of part of dish.

III. Fragment of a carinated handi which has outer projecting rounded rim.

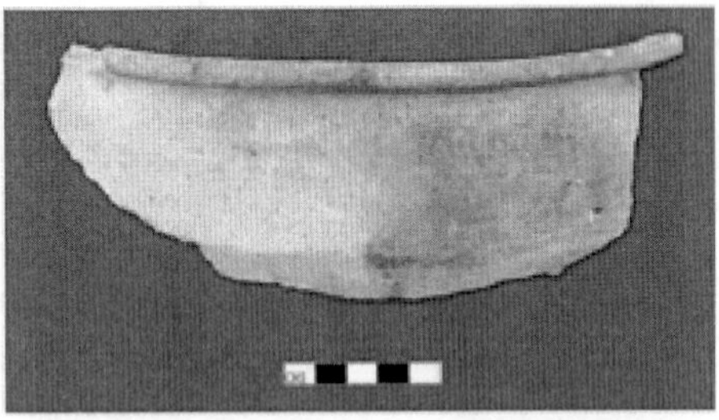

Pl. 42. A sherd of carinated handi.

IV. Glazed Pottery:-Some sherds of local glazed ware or imitation of china glazed ware are found from the south side of the main stupa.

Pl. 43. Sherds of glazed pottery.

V. These sherds are in the form of serving pan with rounded ring like base.

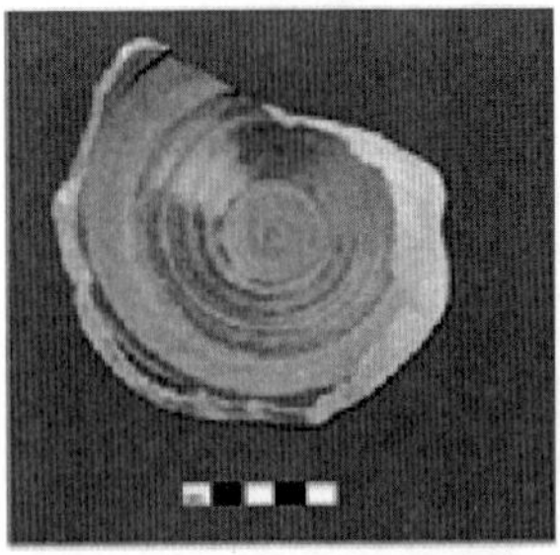

Pl. 44. A sherds of glazed pottery.

Brick size at Nalasopara

For the main stupa there are three sizes of bricks used in the masonry. These are 43 x 23 x 8 cms, 33 x 23 x 8 cms and 35 x 23 x 8 cms. Whereas for the votive stupa sizes are 40 x 23 x 8 cms, 40 x 25 x 8 cms and 30 x 23 x 8 cms. A votive square stupa found at the north side of the main stupa with a 12 courses has the brick size of 25 x 25 x 25 cms.

Description of Brick Size Found at Different Places

Sl. No	Place/District/State	Size of Bricks of Large Stupa in Cms.	Size of Bricks of Votive Stupa in Cms.	References
I	Nalasopara, Palghar/ Maharashtra	43 x 23 x 8 33 x 23 x 8 35 x 23 x 8	40 x 23 x 8 40 x 25 x 8 30 x 23 x 8	Data collected from the field.
II	Stupa No 1, Sanchi, Raisen, Madhy-apradesh	40 x 25 x 7.5		
III	Sarnath, Varanasi, Uttarpradesh	12 x 8.5 x6.5 13 x10 x5 17 x 12 x 5		
IV	Sarai mound, Nal-anda, Bihar	35x24x5 37x27x6 35x27x7		
V	Near Raja Vishal ka Garh, Vasishali, Bihar	38.1 x 22.86 x 5 35.56 x 22.86 x 5 17.78 x 25 x 7	Early Gupta period	
VI	Nalanda		30 x 20 x 5	

Bricks size (CMS)	Periods	References
30 x 20 x 10	Pre Harappan	Encyclopaedia of Indian Archaeology by A. Ghosh, 1989, p.294.
50 to 25 x 25 to 12.5 x 12.5 to 6.35	Harappan	
33 to 27.9 x 15.2 to 12.7 x 12.7 to 8.9	Post-Harappan	
60 to 20 x 31.75 x 16 x 10 to 5	Early Historical	
60 to 11 x 28.6 x 8 x 12 to 4	Late Historical	
43.18 x 27.94 x 3.5	150 BC to 100 AD	Data collected from the field.
55.34 x 28 x 7.62	55 BC	
48.18 x 30.48 x 7.62	100 BC	
43 x 30 x 6	100 BC – 100 AD	
31 x 22 x 5	Late Gupta period	
42 x 28 x 7 41 x26 x 7 39 x 26 x 7	Gupta period	
36 x 27 x 5 38 x 28 x 6 36- 38 x 27-28 x 5- 5.6	Early Gupta period	

5

Investigation of Samples of Bricks, Mortar and Stones found during Scientific Clearance

During the course of restoration of the main stupa and scientific clearance of the surroundings votive stupas, it was felt to investigate the composition of the mortar used in the brick masonry, brick and other material over there. For that Directorate of Science of the Archaeological Survey of India, Dehradun was approached. The sample of the brick, mortar and stones were sent to Dehradun for investigation. The Science branch submitted their report well in time which is being reproduced as under;

The samples of building materials mortar, bricks ancient as well as new modern bricks used in later date conservation and a stone sample were collected for their characterization and understanding their status of preservation. The analysis would enable identification of suitable conservation material to be employes for conservation of the Nalasopara stupa.

The samples were recorded photographically, visually examined for physical observations investigated under microscope.

All the samples were qualitatively analyzed for their salt content. The quantitative elemental composition of the samples was arrived at by X Ray Fluorescence (XRF) instrumental analysis. The mineralogical state of the bricks was analysed with X Ray Diffraction instrumental analysis and the bricks were also analysed with Thermal Gravimetric and Differential Thermal Analysis their firing temperature.

Characterization of Mortar Samples

In all nine samples of mortars were collected from different levels and locations of the Nalasopara stupa. The samples were subjected to instrumental analysis to characterize their physical and chemical composition and status.

Microscopic Examination: Microscopic Examination of all the mortar samples was conducted under zoom stereo microscope. The samples are observed to have amorphous powdery state. The mortar was observed to be constituted of particles with different sizes.

Salt analysis: All the nine samples were found to be mildly acidic with PH ranging from 5.54 to 6.01. The soluble salts of sulphates and nitrates are detected in large amounts in all the nine samples and while the chlorides are detected in moderate quantity.

Particle Size Analysis: The Particle Size Analysis was conducted with motorized sieve shaker as per BIS Standards. The particle size composition detected reveals that all the nine mortar samples have approx. 40% composition of 80 micron size particle, approx. 13% 4.75 mm particle size 15% 1.70 mm particle. The size of very coarse particle is 4.75mm and above, coarse fine sand is between 1.70mm to 80 micron, medium fine sand is between 63 microns to 38 microns and for very fine sand is less than 38 microns. The classification of particles as percentage constituents of the mortar is represented in fig.5

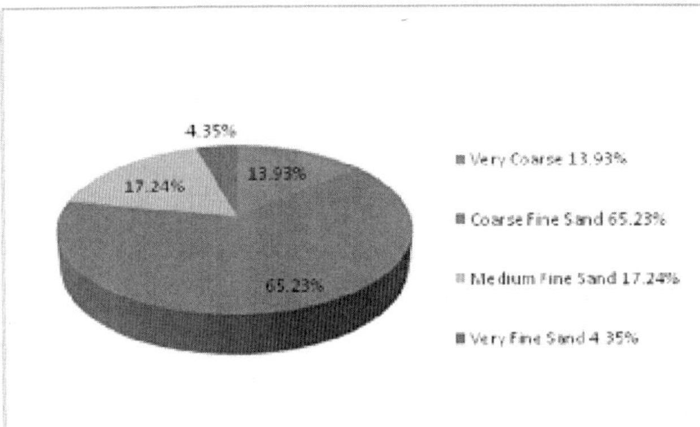

Fig. 5. Classification of Percentage Constituent Particles of Mortar

XRF analysis: The chemical characterization was conducted by XRF instrumental technique with maximum permissible error-2.5% relative. The analysis of all the Mortar samples reveals that the mortar constitutes of high silica content approximately 45%- 48%.

The refractive oxides viz, alumina contents ranging in the all the samples between 11.9% to 12.85%, while Fe203 content ranging in the samples between 14.52% to 16.52% approximately. The calcium oxide content in the mortar is <7.5% and MgO content is analyzed <4.7%.

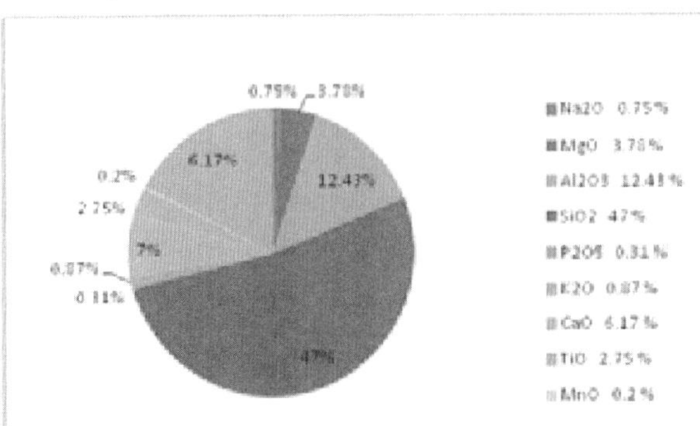

Fig. 6. Elemental Composition of Mortar Sample

Conclusion

The mortar is siliceous mud mortar with very low lime content. The average SiO2 CaO ratio in all the samples being 7:1 approximately. The salt activity in the mortar samples i.e. the sulphates may be attributed to air pollutants while nitrates may be attributed to biological activity and also to proximity to the sea. The chlorides may be due to capillary action of ground water as well as the salt laden sea breeze. The higher nitrate and chlorides in all the samples indicates both capillary phenomena as well as sea breeze impact on the substrates. The high iron content is the reason why mortar is acidic in nature and reddish brown in colour.

Characterization of Brick Samples

A total of eleven samples of bricks were collected from different levels and locations of the Nalasopara Stupa. The samples included nine ancient bricks and two new bricks used in restoration of the stupa site at a later date. All these samples were subjected to instrumental analysis to characterize their physical and chemical composition and status of preservation.

Microscopic Examination: Microscopic Examination of all the brick samples was conducted under zoom stereo Microscopic. The samples are observed to have cavities or air spaces, vegetable fibers and some paddy husk like white colored inclusions. These husk like inclusions are generally observed in all the ancient brick samples. Sample no. 3 is observed to have blackish brown appearance unlike reddish brown colour of all the ancient samples. While in sample no. 12 white chalk coloured inclusions were also observed.

Salt analysis: All the nine ancient brick samples were found to be mildly acidic with pH ranging 6-6.4 except sample no. 10 which has pH 5.53. The soluble salts of nitrates and chlorides are detected in large amounts in all the nine ancient brick samples. While soluble sulphate salts are absent.

The nitrate and chlorides soluble salts are also present in the two new brick samples in large amounts.

XRF analysis: The chemical characterization of the brick samples was conducted by XRF instrumental technique with maximum permissible error- 2.5% relative. The analysis of all the Ancient brick sample reveals that they have similar composition with silica more than 46%- 52% in almost all the samples, Fe_2O_3 content between 16-20% and Al_2O_3 content between from 11-14%

The average percentage elemental constituents of the Ancient bricks is represented in Fig. 7.

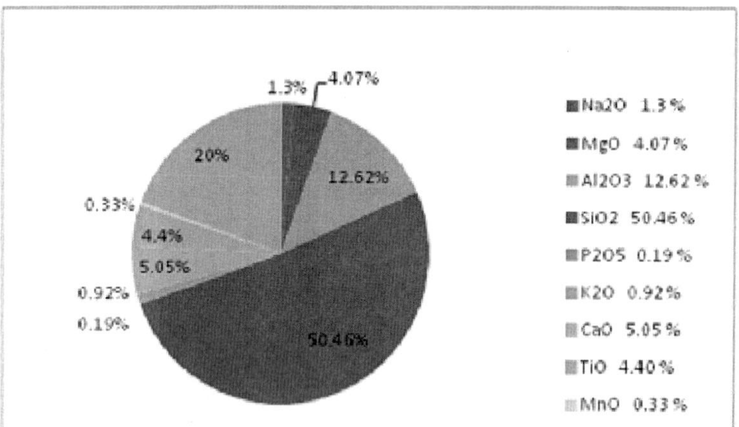

Fig. 7. Elemental Composition of Ancient Brick Sample

The new brick samples have slightly lower silica content, higher Alumina and iron oxide contents than that of ancient bricks. The average percentage elemental constituents of the new bricks is represented in Fig.8

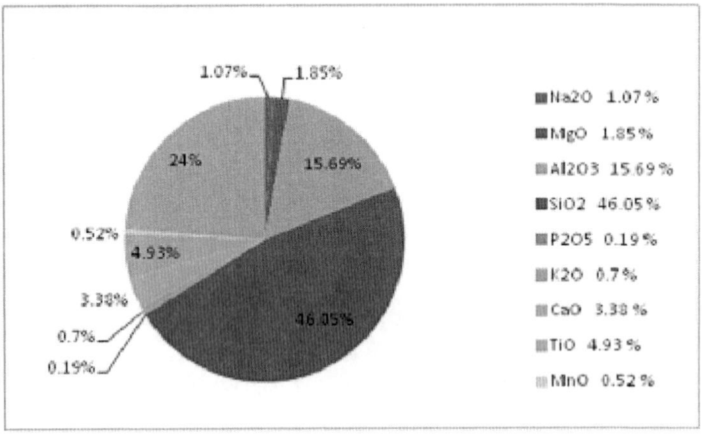

Fig. 8. Elemental Composition of New Brick Sample

Thermal Gravimetric- Differential Thermal Analysis

All the brick samples were subjected to TGA/DTA analysis their firing temperatures. The ancient brick samples are all fired at temperatures more than 850 °C temperature except sample No 4 collected from the location as per photograph 1 which recorded changes at 1026°C and 1159 °C. All other sample show no chemical or thermal change up to 1200 °C temperature.

The new Brick samples collected from location as per photograph 2 used later conservation are analyzed to have different firing temperatures sample 1 firing up to 1200 °C while sample 2 is analyzed to be fired up to 550 °C temperature.

Conclusion: The bricks are siliceous in nature with very low lime content. The average SiO2:CaO ratio in all the sample being 8:1 approximately. The salt activity in the brick in the brick samples i. e. nitrates may be attributed to biological activity as observed in microscopic examination and also to proximity to the sea. The chlorides may be due to capillary action of ground water as well as the salt laden sea breeze. The higher nitrate and chlorides in all the samples indicates both capillary phenomena as well as sea breeze impact on the substrates. The absence of sulphates in the bricks may be due to easy washing away of sulphates from the highly porous brick surface.

The high iron content is the reason why the bricks are reddish brown in colour. The firing temperature and composition of ancient bricks reveals that all the bricks are made from same material source and fired up to 1200 °C except sample 4. The new bricks have varied firing temperature one sample as the ancient bricks while fired at much lower temperatures.

The quantitative chemical constituents of Morter and Bricks, ancient as well as new, samples are similar in nature indicating that the materials have been sourced from the same areas.

Characterization of Stone samples

A Sample of stone was also collected from the Nalasopara Stupa site. The sample was subjected to instrumental analysis to characterize their physical and chemical composition and status of preservation.

Microscopic Examination: Microscopic Examination of the stone sample was conducted under zoom stereo microscopic. The sample was observed to have buff coloured compact mass, with white colored inclusions. The surface is blackish due to accretion of biological material. The stone matrix has shiny inclusions of quartz.

Salt analysis: The stone sample is found to be mildly acidic with ph ranging 6.3. The soluble salts of nitrates and chlorides are detected in large amounts while soluble sulphate salts are absent in the stone sample.

XRF analysis: The chemical characterization of the stone samples was also conducted by XRF instrumental technique with maximum permissible error- 2.5% relative. The analysis of the stone sample reveals the composition with silica content of 58% approx., Fe2O3 content 15% and Al2O3 content 16% approximately.

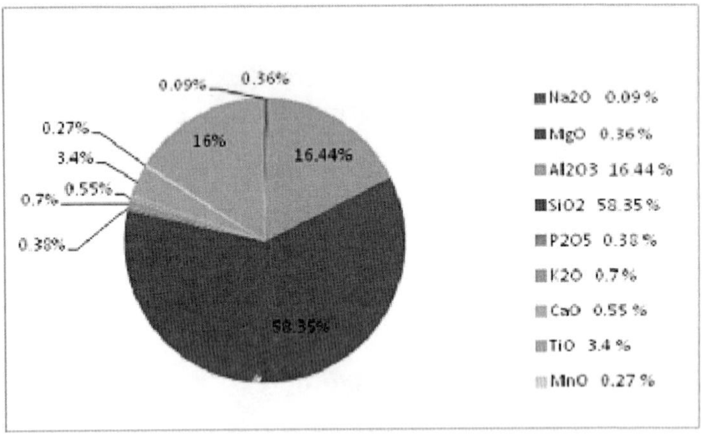

Fig. 9. Elemental Composition of Stone Sample

Conclusion

The Stone is mildly acidic Siliceous in nature with high alumina and iron oxide contents.

6

Monumental Heritage nearby Soparaka (Present Nalasopara)

The most important discovery of Nala Sopara is a broken block of basalt bearing a fragment of one of Asoka's edicts which was found near the Bhatela pond to the east of the town close to the old landing-place. The inscriptions are in six lines in the Asokan character, which, if compared with other copies of Asoka's edicts, proved to be a part of the eighth edict. The dark letters are those preserved on the Sopara stone, the other letters are filled from the Girnar and other edicts. The copy shows that the fragment is about one-third of the original edict.The fourteen or fifteen edicts of Asoka which have been discovered in Girnar, Kapuredi-gadi, Kalsi, Dhauli, and Jaugada, have always been found in a group. In no case have separate edicts inscribed in or near Sopara.

Vasai Fort

Situated on the sea-coast about 48 km north of Bombay and at the mouth of Ulhas Creek in Vasai . The present fort was once an independent island now adjoining with the mainland of Vasai.

Vasai fort was constructed by Bahadur Shah, the sultan of Gujarat (AD 1526-27) and it was fortified by Malik Taughan, in AD 1552. In AD 1739 it was taken over by the Peshwa Bajirao-I and was finally passed in the hands of the British in 1817 AD.

A stone with a Portuguese inscription near the gateway records that, 'During the reign of the most high and most mighty King Dom Joam of Portugal, the third of this name, and when D. Afonso de Noronha, son of the Marquis of Villa Real, was Viceroy, and Francisco de Sa, Captain of the fort and city of Bacai, this bastion named Sam Sebastian, was built on the 22nd February 1554'. In an another inscription recorded at the citadel wall of the fort states that, 'The first Captain who built this fortress was Garcia de Sa, by command of the Governor Nuno da Cunha in the year 1536'.

This fort was one of the most significant forts of the Portuguese who made their main base here for North Konkan. The fort comprised of eleven bastions, two main entrances and a postern. The fort complex includes six churches, four convents, two colleges (a Jesuit and a Franciscan), a citadel, two palaces, a pond, a tank, temples, several smaller structures and some mounds bearing buried structures. Besides that the remains of straight streets and large squares, a regular planning feature of most European towns are still in extant. The different names are given to the bastions of the fort by the Portuguese such as Nossa Senhora dos Remedios, Thiago, Sam Joao, Cavalerios, Sebastian, Paulo, Pedro, Elefanta, Madre de Rens, Reis Magos and Goncalo and were typically of the four-sided ear-shaped jutting typology common for Portuguese forts. The two double gateways were the west entrance from the land called the Porta Da Terra and Porta Do Mar or the sea gate on the east, along with a small postern on the south leading to the koli settlement. This fort was protected by the ASI during pre-independence through a notification no 2704 – A, dated 26.05.

Bolinj

The monument is located about 20Kms from Vasai. In the name of monument here is only a small water tank with signs of steps on its southern side and some large architectural blocks on the south. An embellished sculpture of Vishnu has been recovered from here. Site was protected by the archaeological Survey of India in 1938 vide notification no. F.18-22 / 37-F. D., dated 25.03.1938.

Ambernath Temple

This monument is situated 7 km southeast of Kalyan. The temple of Ambarnath is in Bhumija style dated to AD 1060 according to an inscription. It was built in basalt stone during the reign of the Silahara dynasty. Originally the temple had a walled enclosure. The temple consists of a garbhagriha, ardhamandapa and sabha mandapa with three porches on the north, south and west. The sabamandapa consists of a central square, which is surrounded by aisles and passage on the four sides. The east passage leads to the garbhagriha through ardhamandapa. The garbhagriha enshrines a shivalinga on sunken yonipitha. Each part of the temple viz pillars, wall, niches, doorframe and ceilings including its exterior and interior wall are profusely festooned with the images of gods and goddesses, subordinate deities, dikpalas, dwarapara, musicias, dancers, nymphs, animals including foliated and geometrical motifs. Temple was protected by the ASI vide notification no. 2704 – A, dated 26.05.1909.

Arnala Fort

Arnala fort is approximately 40 km. from Thane city and 14.49 km north of Vasai. It was also called the Illha de Vaccas, or cow's island by the Portuguese. Arnala is a compact fort built on an island 0.25 km. off the Agashi coast and was also known as Janjira after the Marathi corruption of the Arabic word 'Jazirah' meaning an island. Commanding the southern and main entrance to the Vaitarna river, the most extensive inlet in north Konkan, Sultan Mahmud Begada constructed Arnala fort in 1516. Occupation by the Portuguese in 1530, meant destruction of several Saracenic structures within the fort, but the fort itself seems to be largely retained. A guard of soldiers was stationed at the fort, which also has an extension in the form of a round bastion like structure at the south of the main fort looking out over the Vaitarna Creek inlet at the south. Arnala became a major naval depot during the Portuguese times and served as an intermediate outpost between Vasai in the south and Daman in the north, acting also as a bulwark protecting the mouth of Vaitarna Creek. Among north Konkan forts it ranked next to Vasai in size and strength, and was superior to Vasai in the uniform breadth of its rampart top, or terrepleine, and its uniform line of defense. Some amount of ship building activity also took place at Arnala. After an intense battle between the Portuguese and the Marathas in 1739, Arnala was captured by the Marathas and according to a Marathi inscription over the northern gateway, was rebuilt during the reign of Peshwa Bajirao I by an architect named Baji Tulaji. Efforts for its capture were made by the British in 1781, when the Marathas did not yield and preparations for bombardment of Arnala were made from Agashi. It was briefly occupied by the British at this time when the East India Company troops captured it under Colonel Goddard, but was returned to the Peshwas and finally came under the dominion of the British in 1817. Constituting a compact fort, Arnala consists of a more or less rectangular fortified complex with gateways on the centre of each side, the main one being the north entrance. The fort complex, apart from the ancillary bastion at a short distance on the south and the actual ramparts, comprises of an original but ruinous structure, two temples, a Muslim dargah, a miniature shrine housing the local deities, an old octagonal well and 4 other wells.

Gas

It is located in Nala Sopara. Gas was originally believed to be the site of the old town of Sopara and yielded many archaeological evidences in the form of fragments of stone and relic mounds, indicating its historicity.

The ancient mound locally known as Sonar Bhat, approximately rises to about 6 feet height from the ground level. The top surface of the mound seems to have been partly unearthed remains of a small tank probably of the 14th century A.D. Pottery is also found embedded in the section, which also do not help to throw light on its cultural assemblage Besides two wells and a reservoir still in extant are at the east and northeast part of the site respectively. Records indicate the location of a broken cross-legged figure of Ambika, at the east foot of the mound, as well as close to it large earthenware cups were also unearthed from here. The Chakreshwar bull (from the Chakreshwar temple in the vicinity) was dug out of a well about 50 yards to the west. Near the road-side a damaged sculptured stone was also found, the main figure in which was perhaps the Sun, as he held a lotus in each hand, apparently part of an entrance door of the 11th or 12th century. A part section is visible but the proper cultural aspects of the site could not be ascertained.. Unfortunately it is rather difficult to find out the sequence or the potentialities of this mound in the absence of a clear section. This monument was protected by the ASI vide no F-18-22 / 37-F, dated 25.03.1938.

7

Inscription Finding Names of Soparaka

In the caves of Karle, Kanheri, Naneghat and Nasik the name of Sopara had mentioned. In **Karle cave: 1.** out of 22 inscriptions, two (inscription no 8 and 9) associats to the Soparaka wherein names of Satimita, Dhammutaray, Nanda and Sopara had referred. On the shaft of pitch pillar on the north side of name occurred inscription as below;

"Soparaka bhayataan dhamuttara-s
-yaan samaanthas theras (Maa)-
Tulas antewaasis bhaan-
Kas nandaputis saatimitas
Saha(maataapi) tuya thamo daanmulam.

The gift of the cost of a pillar by satimita from Soparaka, out of respect for his maternal uncle the bhadanta Dhamutaraya, by his disciple and sister's son Satimita, the son of Nanda, with his mother and father (Burgess: 1881; p.31-33).

This inscription has been engraved on the shaft of the fifth pillar on the left or north side of the cave.

2:- Soparaka bhayataan dhamuttaryaan bhaan-
Kas saatimitas.
Sasariro thamo daanam.

There is a hole cut for the purpose of holding a relic in the centre of lotus carved on the front of the pillar just where the inscription end (Burgess: 1881 ;p.33).

In Kanheri caves :-

> "Tathaha soparakam gachchejjamadagnya nisevitam
> Ramatirtha naraha snatva vindyad
> Bahusuwarnakam" (Gokhle: 1991, p.45).

Sopara , the capital city of Soparahara in the Satvahana period was the cultural centre in ancient times. In the Nasik inscription as above, of Nahapana , Ramatirtha of Sopara has been mentioned as a holy place which is mentioned in the Mahabharata too.

Siddhama upasakasaa vinumitasaa nigamasaa mundapalasaa. Soparakasaa saha kutubinihi sahaa balake, hi Deyaddhamma chhetam dinama akhayaanivi. (Gokhle: 1991, p.75).

The inscription record a permanent gift of a field by the merchant Mundapala the son of upasaka Vinhumita alongwith his wife and children.

8

Other Monuments of Great Archaeological Significance

Bedsa Caves

Bedsa (Pl.45 and Fig 10) being located in a strategic place nearer the trade routes linking the konkan ports and inland towns, it began to gain importance gradually and shortly afterwords in the early part of the 1st century BC.It is located 35Kms North-West of Pune in the hillock overlooking the broad valley of the river Pavna. Caves can be approached from the village by travelling west and climbing a steep flight of steps which leads to a wide flat ledge of the trap hill. The caves facing east are excavated from south to north. It has a monastic establishment with fifteen excavations in all. Only two of them, the great chaitya hall 7 and cave 11 are architecturally noteworthy. The others include two small chaityagriha caves 1, 3 and caves 10 and 12 are unfinished. Beside that other antiquity includes cisterns and inscription. On the basis of one inscription, found in the cave no. 7, this place can be identified as marakuda .In the course of about a century since the beginning of this monastic establishment it becomes a holy place.

Pl. 45. Chaitya of Bedsa caves.

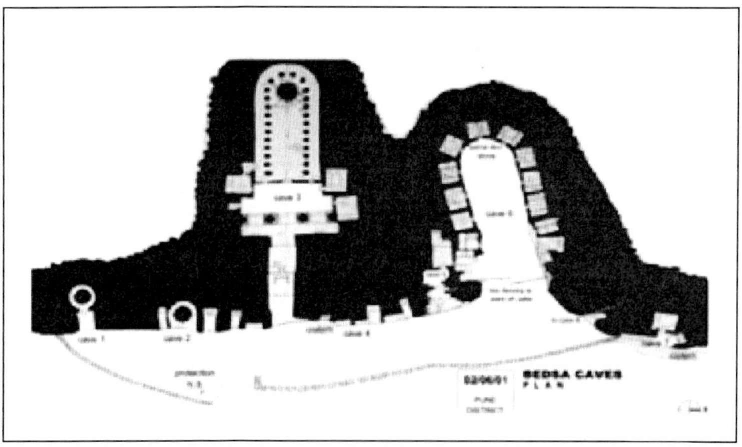

Fig. 10. Site plan of Bedsa caves. Dist Pune.

A disciple of a thera created here a chaitya shrine (cave no 3) in honour of his teacher. The monastic establishment at Bedsa, the ancient marakuda, appears to have enjoyed patronage hardly for about a century and a half. While the monastery could have continued to be in use in later times, but there is no evidence of architectural activity at the place after about the 1st century AD. Being a site of great archaeological significance it was notified by the govt. of British India as a monument of national importance vide no.2704-A, dated 26.05.1909.

Bhaja Caves

Bhaja (Pl.46, Fig. 11) group of caves consists of 22 excavations. Itis one of the important Buddhist centers of Hinayana faith in Maharashtra located on a hill near Bhaja village, Maval Taluka in district Pune. The river Indrayani is located nearby and waters the valley. The excavations consist of Chaityagriha, viharas and water cisterns. They are excavated on a scrap of the hill at a height of 120 mtrs from above the surrounding plains and all faces West. The most prominent among the excavations is the Chaityagriha. The Chaityagriha is considered to be the earliest of its kind and a close copy of wooden proto type. On plan it consist of a large apsidal hall divided into a central nave and side aisles divided by 27 pillars in two straight row which forms a semi circle at the back. A stupa is placed at the back for worship. Cave No.18 is a monastery and consists of a rectangular hall with a front pillared verandah.

Pl. 46. Front view of Bhaja caves.

Fig. 11. Plan of Bhaja Caves dist. Pune.

The verandah of this monastery has two famous sculptural reliefs which are most important. One depicts a royal personage attended by two women, driving in a chariot driven by four horses, which tramples on a demonic figure. The person in royal attire has been identified by some scholars as Surya. To the left of the door is depicted a person driving an elephant carrying an ankusha, with attendants carrying a banner and spear. The figure has been identified by some as Indra. From the sculptural point of view this cave is imperative as seven panels of human figurines here in different location of the wall reveals information on the attributes, ornamentation and different poses of figurines. Apart from Cave 18 have other monasteries of simple type. Some exceptions are also noticeable, like the ones with a circular cell and a stupa inside; circular cell with oblong verandah etc. An inscription datable to 2nd century AD is found on the back wall of a cistern records the donation of Maharathi Kosikiputa Vishnudata. Another two inscriptions inscribed on the wooden beam below the vault are short and dedicatory in nature and datable to 2nd century BC. The survival of this original inscription on the wooden beams indicates that they have survived for the past 2200 years.The caves are datable from century 2nd BC to AD 2nd. However the group was under occupation up to 5-6th century AD as attested from some of the painted Buddha images in the Chaityagriha. As richness in finishing of Chaityagriha, smoothness of stupa and sculptural embellishment, this site was notified as a monument of national importance by the British India vide no.2704-A, dated 26.05.1909.

Junnar Caves

The presence of largest number of rock cut excavations and inscriptions make Junnar a prominent site for the study of rock cut architecture and palaeography. The cave groups in Junnar taluka, district Pune locates at a distance of 96 kms from Pune and on the southern bank of river Kukdi. The Junnar range is encircled by a series of hills on all sides, namely, Shivaneri and Tulja hills on the west; the Sulaiman on the north and east; Manmodi on the south. It is near to Naneghat, an ancient vital pass in the western ghats which connects the sea ports of Sopara, Kalyan and Thana, with the cities and towns of the mainland like Nasik, Paithan and Ter, etc. Junnar has the largest number of rock cut excavations numbering over 200 independent excavations spread over the four hills namely Tulja, Manmodi, Shivaneri and Lenyadri group of caves.

All the excavations belongs to the Hinayana phase and are datable from 2nd century B.C. to late 3rd century A.D. The 24 inscriptions found within the caves provide useful paleographical data for the relative dating of the caves.

Pl. 47. Front View of Tulja bhawani caves.

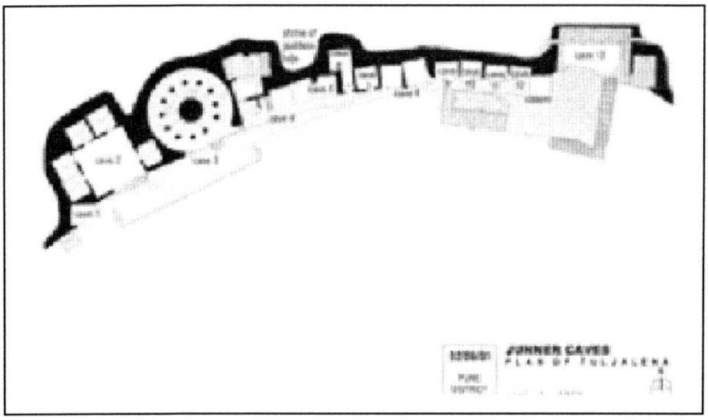

Fig. 12. Site plan of Tuljabhawani caves.

These inscriptions reveal name of donors including members of the royal family as well as commoners, which also includes Yavanas (Greeks). One particular inscription from the Manmodi group mentions the name of a minister of Maharathi Nahapana (AD 119-124). This site was protected as a monument of national importance vide n. 2704-A, dated 26.05.1909.

Kanheri Caves

Kanheri caves (Pl.48, Fig.13); one of the largest excavations hewn out in a single hillock of Borivali locates north of central Mumbai at Sanjay Gandhi National Park Borivali in sub urb of Mumbai. This group of caves includes more than 110 caves, more than 100 inscriptions, cisterns, sculptures, votive stupas, remains of old dame, paintings and other antiquities revealing three important phases of Hinayana,Mahayana and vajrayayana sects of Buddhist. Its large establishment indicate its popularity as a monastic establishment and pilgrim centre, and its importance as heightened by the fact that it is the only centre where a continuous progression of Buddhist faith and architecture is observed as an unbroken legacy right from 2nd century BC. to 10th century AD. Some scholar considers its ancientness from 3rd century BC. (cave no. 4 stupa) .

Kanheri consists of excavations primarily undertaken during the Hinayana phase but later on Mahayana stylistic architecture as well as few paintings of the Vajrayana order came in prevalence too.

Pl. 48. Front view of Kanheri caves.

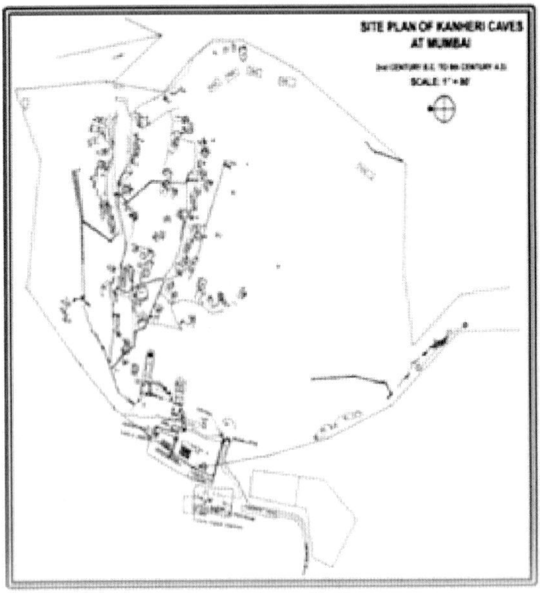

Fig. 13. Site plan of Kanheri caves, dist Mumbai Sub.

Considering the long and enduring patronage of Kanheri, however the most prosperous period of its development coincides with the rule of the Shatakarni kings (BC. 200 – AD. 350), especially the reign of Gotamiputra II (A.D. 177–196) or Gotamiputra Yajnashri Shatakarni. Of the 110 excavations extant at Kanheri, most of them are carved in a simple form of the vihara and chaitya, with some of them displaying outstanding values such as cave no. 2 or the almonry cave, cave no. 3 or main chaitya cave, cave no. 11 (old no. 10) or the durbar cave, stupa burial gallery or cave no. 84 (old no. 38), cave no. 67 (old no. 35), etc are unique caves in addition to the dam, external courts, rock-cut benches and water system. Site was notified as a monument of national importance vide no2704 - A, dated 26.05.1909.

Karla Caves

Karla (Pl. 49, Fig.14) known by its ancient name as 'Veluraka' is situated in Maval Taluka, Lonavalaon Pune-Mumbai highway, about 60 km northwest of Pune. The caves are excavated nearly 100 mtrs above a high spur of chain of hills on the north flank of the Indrayani valley. It is on the ancient highway connecting sea ports of Kalyan and Sopara to the cities located inland.

The group at Karla consists of 16 rock cut excavations of which cave No. 8 is the chaityagriha and one of the grandest of all the chaitagrihas ever found in the country so far.

The detailed tracery in the caves were enhanced during the Satvahana rulers. The caves, like other Buddhist caves of Maharashtra, were caused from the donations and support of different groups of then society. The inscriptions found here clearly reveals of 27 individuals from various places like Vejamti (Banavasi, north Kanara district, nearly 600 km south of Karla); Sopara (nearly 100 km northwest of Karla) and unidentified towns of Umehanakata and Dhenukakata. Most of the donors from Dhenukakata were Yavanas.

Pl. 49. Front view of Karle Caves.

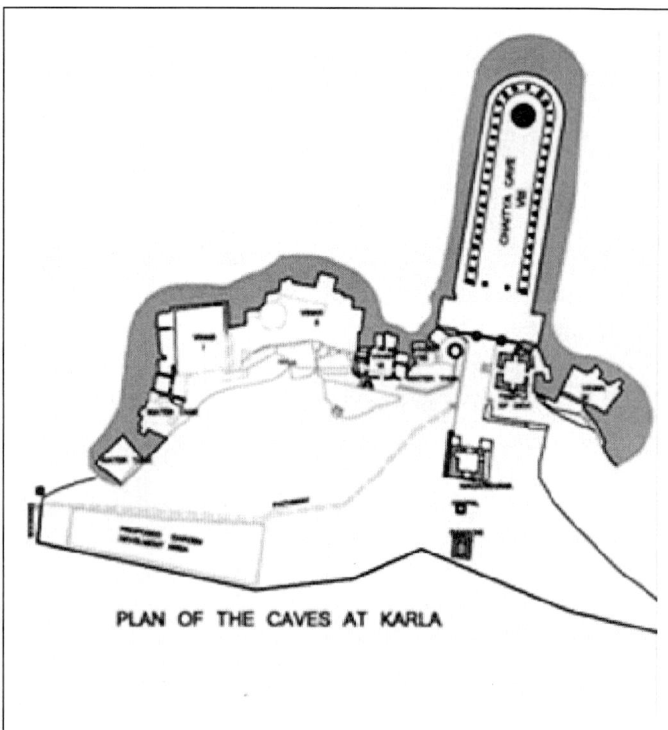

Fig 14. Site plan of Karle Caves, dist. Pune.

Chaityagriha here consists of an apsidal hall with a front verandah. The apsidal hall is divided into a nave and two aisles by two rows of pillars which meet at the rear behind the stupa in a semicircle forming the apse. It can be entered through a screen wall erected in front of the verandah, which in turn has three entrances, the central one opening into the nave and the other two, into the flanking aisles. The side walls of the verandah and inner face of the screen wall are extensively decorated with sculptures. The front wall of the verandah is also profusely decorated which is executed in two parts. The lower portion consists of a row of railing pattern and above which is six mithuna figures rising up to the level of lintels. The portion above the doorways is decorated with a series of miniature chaitya windows imitating the huge chaitaya window. These miniature windows are connected through a vedika and a roll cornice. This pattern extends throughout the entire width of the facade of the hall. The pillars are executed with great ingenuity and vigor which reflect the sculptural art of the period. The roof of the aisles is flat, while the pillars of the nave support a simple architrave over which rises a barrel vaulted roof which ends in a semi-dome over the stupa in the rear. This roof is fitted with actual wooden curved ribs and longitudinal rafters.

However, from the 7th century AD, when the Mahayana became more popular with their liberal thoughts, the later Karla caves do present the Buddha in his physical form such as the Buddha preaching while seated on a lion-supported throne, along with magnificent carvings of three elephants. Its earliest date is assigned by the scholar as 2end century BC whereas some says 3rd century BC.

On the basis of its archaeological potential, caves are notified by the government of India as a monument of national importance vide no.2704 - A, dated 26.05.1909.

Kondavite Caves

Located at Andheri in sub urb of Mumbai, this cave (Pl. 50, Fig. 15) complex is momentous from evolution point of view. Also called Mahakali cave, this cave complex comprises of two rows, Group I of fifteen caves on southeast face and Group II of four caves on the northwest face. Of them Cave no. 9 is noteworthy and most interesting in terms of its unique plan which place this cave among the category of oldest caves of India (3rdcentury BC).

It comprises of a veranda, of which the front wall is broken and only a few dowels in the floor survive, the cave leads to a stupa that is enclosed in a hut-like enclosure which corresponds with the Barabar caves of Bihar.

Pl. 50. A view of Kondavite caves.

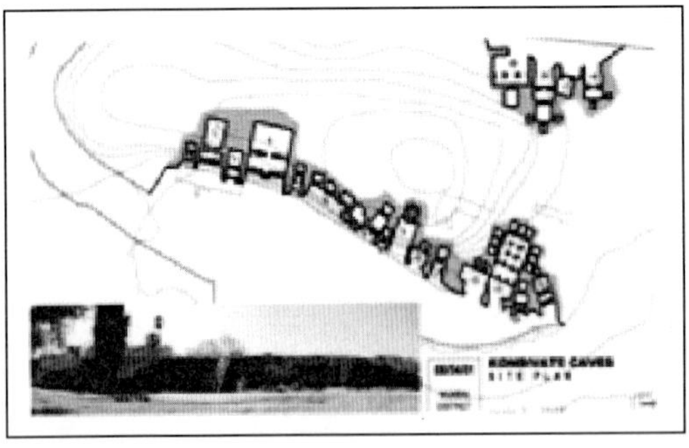

Fig. 15. Site plan of Kondavite caves, dist Mumbai Sub urb.

This enclosure of the stupa within the chamber, with a circumambulation path gives rise to the introduction of a semi-circular wall along the stupa. The stupa is devoid of ornamentation except railing pattern at mid-level with dowels at the top for a chattri. Its thick wall around the stupa has a central door with a latticed window on either sides. Over the right window is a two line Pali inscription recording, "Gift of a vihar, with his brother, by Pittimba a Brahman of the Gotamas gotra, and inhabitant of Pachi Kama". Other caves are simple. Group II caves, comprising of four caves, directly face the road and settlement on the north west, probably from the 4th or 5th century. This cave was notified by the government of India as a monument of national importance vide no.2704 - A, dated 26.05.1909.

Naneghat Caves and Inscriptions

Naneghat (Pl.51, Fig. 16) is well known for Satavahana inscriptions. Located 305 kms south of Mumbai and 140 kms east from Pune, Naneghat caves are nearest to the Junnar whence one can reach this site about 34 kms west by pucca motorable road. Divided naturally by a deep dike this place geographically indicates a boundary demarcation from one region to another. The people coming from Konkan used to come to kalyana through this pass.

Architecturally, caves are simple and devoid of any decoration of them one (main cave) cave contains inscriptions on the three walls which are full of description about Satvahana king. The garish account of various sacrifices like ashvamedha, rajasuya and Vajappeya conducted by the king Satakarni and his consort Naganika are mentioned here. Inscriptionsare like a pedigree wherein Satakarni is referred as prithviyah prathamavira (only warrior in the world). After the performance of sacrificial rituals a fees to the priest were given in the form of Karsapana.

The other names in the inscription referred are; Simuka Satvahana (founder of dynasty), Devi Naganika, Sri Satakarni, Kumara Bhaya, Maharathi Tranakayira, Kumara Hakusri and Kumara Satavahana. These inscriptions are engraved by king Vedishri who as a king of Dakshinapath probably improved Nana pass. The other name like Simuka was his grandfather and Shri Satkarni and queen Naganika his parents while kumara Hakushri and Kumara Satavahana was his two sons (Gazetteer;1885; 212-13). In the beginning salutations are offered to Dharma, Indra, Chandra, Surya, Agni, Marut, Yama, Varuna, Kubera, Vasava, Sankarshana and Vasudeva (Gazetteer; 1885; 212-13). After the fall of great Maurya dynasty, Satavahana flourished dominantly from 1st Century BC to 3rd century AD and swayed upto trans-Vindhyan region and claimed themselves the lord of dakshinapath. There capital was paithan (Pratishthana) near present Aurangabad district in Maharashtra.

Naneghat group contains total seven caves, ten cisterns, inscriptions, sculptures and remains of old structures. Main cave is plain without decoration and only noteworthy because of inscriptions dedicated to Satavahana king Satakarni and his family. It consists of a flamboyant records of inscriptions revealing detail information on the king's family, praise of combatant Satakarni, sacrifices performed by him and his wife Naganika and obeisance of vedic deity.

On the backside of the wall has the remains of feets and level inscription underneath, which indicates that the stone images of Satavahana family were installed inside the cave now disappeared due to mutilation. The inscriptions are carved on the all sides of the wall specifically lateral sides. Just in front of the main cave has an another plain cave mutilated on fronton.

Pl. 51. View of Naneghat caves.

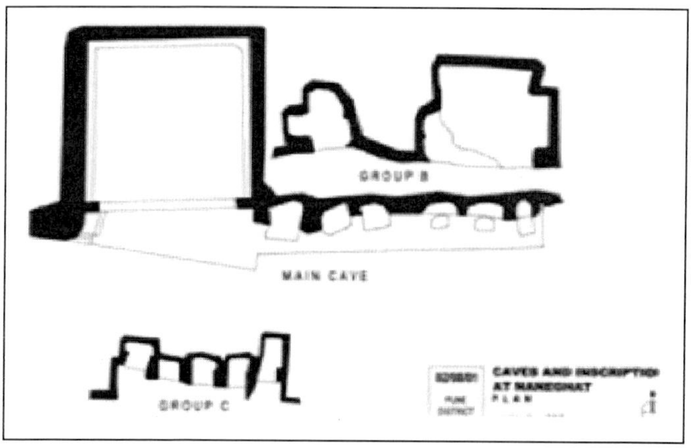

Fig 16. Site plan of Nane ghat Caves, dist. Pune.

Five other caves are towards north side just above the dike leading to main cave at left side. These are simple and small niche like caves carved in parallel to each other. It is not known whether these are meant for enshrining image inside or constructed for residential purpose. But, since the evidence of their fore parts extension are also there in mutilated form so it can be assumed that these might had built for residential purpose. It appears that most of the sculptures from the site was either taken away or mutilated as witnessed from the images of main caves. In spite of that few sculptures like remains of feet, stone pitch place north of the main cave at the right side of pathway, a stone grinder and a sculpture of gajalaxmi placed quite away toward north on the rubble platform, are still in existence and reveals valuable information of the past.

North side of the dike has a great platue surrounded all around by the beautiful range of mountains indicating probability of old settlements. The evidence of residential structures and few sculptures and fragment still exists over there. Of them Gajalakxmi is placed on a rubble platform for worshipping by the local peasants.

Naneghat inscription is one among the oldest inscriptions of India which gives flamboyant information like those of Ashokan inscriptions found in different parts of the country. Its like a pedigree which not only state about the velour of the satavahana kings but show a deep faith in the Brahmanism and indicate that during the time of 90 BC Buddhism was not only flourishing but Brahamanism too was simultaneously running parallel to the former.

1st century BC to 2nd Century AD was the period of renaissance for the growth of trade between India and Roman empire. A vivid reference comes in the account of Periplus of the Erythrean Sea about the trade and trade centers in the Western part of the country like Bharukacchah, Sopara, Kalyana, Muziris, Paithan and ter. These centers were linked together for brisk trade.

The caves and other antiquarian remains of Naneghat are of archaeological potential therefore site was protected by the Archaeological Survey of India as a monument of national vide no. 6460, dated 26.06.1929.

Shelarwadi Caves

Located on the old Mumbai-Pune road about 125 kms south-east of Mumbai and 32 kms north-west of Pune in district Pune, the group of caves of shelarwadi (Pl. 52, Fig.17) nestled in a picturesque garodi hills a sub range of sahayadri at the right bank of river pauna. About 3 kms south west of Talegaon it can be reached by walk from main road of Mumbai-Pune, then after bifurcating from main road one has to reach through stiff climbing by a kachcha and stepped pathway.

On the hillock, Cave no. I is quite ahead and above the pathway leading to main cave. It can be approached through the steps hewn out to the rock. The cave is preceded by a rectangular courtyard without pillars. This courtyard has provided with niche at the lateral side which appears not for enshrining the sculptures but for sitting purpose. The courtyard opens inside into the two cells through separate plain doors.

Pl. 52. A view of Shilarwadi caves,

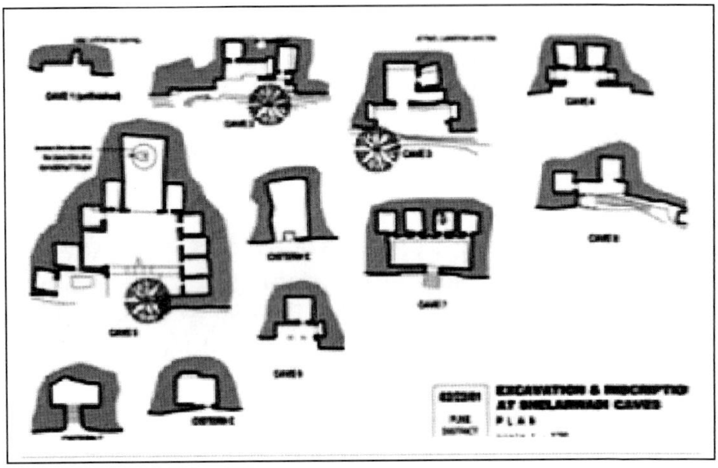

Fig 17. Plan of Shilarwadi caves, dist Pune.

The main group consists of three caves. Of them two are hewn out independently and preceded by a cistern and broken courtyard while the other one (main) has excavated at left side. There was an open courtyard of the former caves which has now broken and only small portion of it only exists. At the upper right corner of the entrance has an inscription in brahami. In the years back this cave appears converted into shaivite by installing a Shivaling inside the center cell. It can be entered by two doorways leading to a courtyard which further opens into six cells; three each at lateral sides and three at back side of them center one, quite wide, was probably enshrined with a stupa but now with shiva linga canopied by metal serpent. This can be witnessed with a harmika(stepped pyramid); an upper part of stupa which still exists on the ceiling above the present enshrined shiva linga.

All the cells inside main cave are plain and without any decoration and motifs. Only at the upper part of the backside cell; right to the sanctum has an inscription carved in brahami.

The sanctum which is almost square in size has a pedestal built at the center of the floor over which rests a shivalinga coiled up by metal serpent all around. The pedestal for the shivalinga has provided additionally after excavating the floor at a depth of around 6-8 inch below the floor level. This creation is a latter addition. The original plan of the cave reveals a large courtyard in front of the cells which were surrounded by four cells at the left sides, four at the right and three at the back side but later on one additional wall of dressed rubble had created at the fronton keeping one each cell from both sides separated out of the courtyard.

There is no carving and decoration inside the caves except one stepped pyramid (*harmika*) on the ceiling that is upper most part of stupa which might have existed over here before shiva linga.

Cave no.3 has only one niche at left side provided for sitting purpose. The cell inside is small and plain.

Cave no.4 has a small cave approached by a flight of steps leading to a rectangular courtyard which further opens into the two plain cells through two doors. This is the only cave in Shelarwadi wherein pilasters and upper part of the wall between courtyard and cells are decorated. The pilasters are decorated with elephants, lion and *vyala* capital which indicates Hinayanic traits of the cave. The upper parts of the walls between courtyard and cells, touching ceilings, are decorated with *vedika* (railing) designs however the wall supported with pilasters in between has provided with pilasters.

Pilasters of the cave no IV are octagonal of which shaft rests on kumbha pedestaled with stepped pyramid. The upper part of pilaster has composed of reverted bell, beads row, three membered pattika for surmounting animal figurines. The capitals are decorated with elephant, lion and vyala figurines.

Cave No.5 is opposite to the cave no.I. Both the caves has no courtyard but opens separately through plain doors through Like other caves, it has the same plan consisting of a rectagular courtyard whence one can reach two different cells by two plain doors.The cells are plain without any decoration. Both the cells are now enshrined with modern statues of vithoba.

There are total four inscriptions in the caves of Shelarwadi carved separately on the top wall of the doors. The first inscription in prakrit has on the top of entrance of one of the independent cave outside of main cave.The inscription, badly rubed up, is of five lines while the letters are improportionately carved out.

Another prakrit inscriptions are inside the main cave above the door of right cell. More clear than the former it has composed in four lines on whole space of lintel of the cell.

Cave No.2; I:-On the top of right entrance of independence cell out side main.

II:-Inside main cave.

On the cave no. 4 there are also two inscription on both the top side of main door. Both these inscription corresponds to the deformed Hindi and appears of modern period.

By the name of"Excavation and inscription at Shelarwadi caves" this site was notified by the Notification No. 2704-A dated 26.4.1909 as a monument of national importance.

Shelarwadi was surveyed by Burgess (Virachand: 2012; 188).Under the aegis of the Bombay Branch of the Royal Asiatic Society, the Cave Temples Commission was established in 1848 under the chairmanship of John Wilson. In November 1860 when the CTC submitted detailed report on the caves studied among them were Shilarwadi caves. The report listed work done by Pandit Vishnu Shastri on the caves and inscription including 18 in Karla, 2 in Bhaja, 2 Bedsa,1 Shelarwadi, 2 Naneghat, 24 Junnar, 9 Nasik, 4 Ajanta, 20 at Kanheri, and 5 at Mahad caves were transcripted and deciphered (Virachand: 2012;80-81).

Bibliography

Primary Sources

Tripitaka

Books

Ambedkar, B.R. (2011)The Buddha and his dharma.

Cunningham, Alexander (1854) The bhilsa topes or Buddhist Monuments of Central India, reprint 1997, New Delhi

Burgess, J. and Bhagwandas Indarji (1881) Inscriptions from the cave temples of western India, ASI.

Dharmasey, Virchand (2012) Bhagwanlal Indraji the First Indian Archaeologist; multidisciplinary approach to the study of past, Darshak Itihas Nidhi Gujarat.

Fergusson, James and James Burgess (1880) The Cave Temples of India, Delhi.

Goenka, S. (1995) Tipitakameinsamyanksambuddh, Igatpuri.

Gokhle, Shobhna (1991) Kanheri Inscriptions.

Vipashyanavishodhanvinyas,reprint 2002.

Goenka, S. (2009) Mahamanava Buddha ki mahan Vidya; Vipasyana ka Udgam aur Vikas.

Goenka, S.(2011)The great Buddha's noble teachings, the origin and spread of Vipasana.

Hardy, Spencer R. (1853) A Manual of Buddhism.

Indraji, Bhagwanlal (1882) Antiqairrian remains at Sopara and Padana.

Kail, O. C. (1975) Buddhist Cave Temples of India, Bombay.

Law, B.C, (1954) Historical Geography of Ancient India.

Mitra, Debala (1971) Buddhist Monuments, Calcutta.

Motichandra (1977)Trade and trade routes in Ancient India, Motilal Banarsidas, New Delhi.

Nagaraju, S. (1981) Buddhist Architecture of Western India, Delhi.

Sankrityayana, Rahul (1952) Bauddha Samskriti.

Gazetteers

Pathak, A. S. (1882) Gazetteer of the Bombay Presidency – Thana Places of Interest, Facsimile Reproduction,Vol. XIV, Bombay, (reprinted 2000).

Pune District Gazetteer (Bombay 1885).

Thana District Gazetteer (rev. 2006).

Remaining Figures

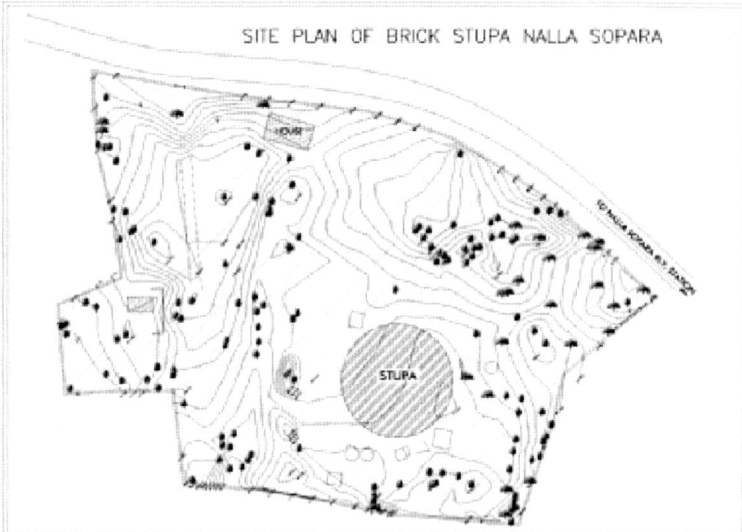

Fig. 18. Contour map of Barund Rajacha kot.

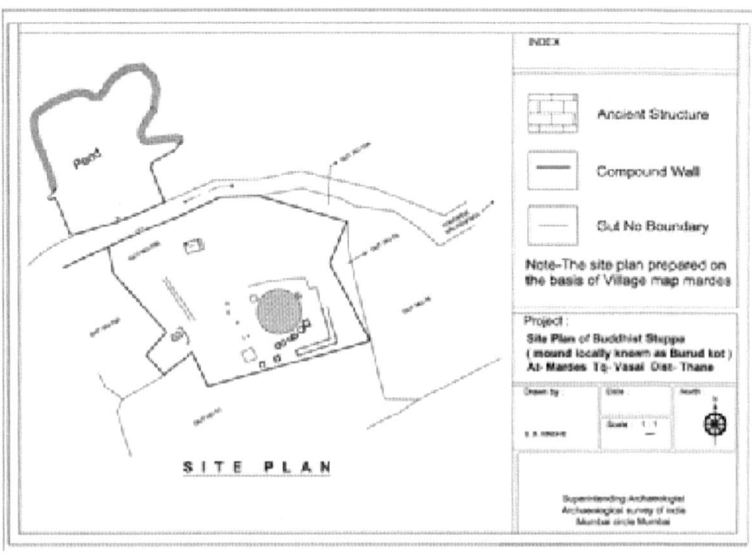

Fig. 19. Site plan of Barund Rajacha kot.

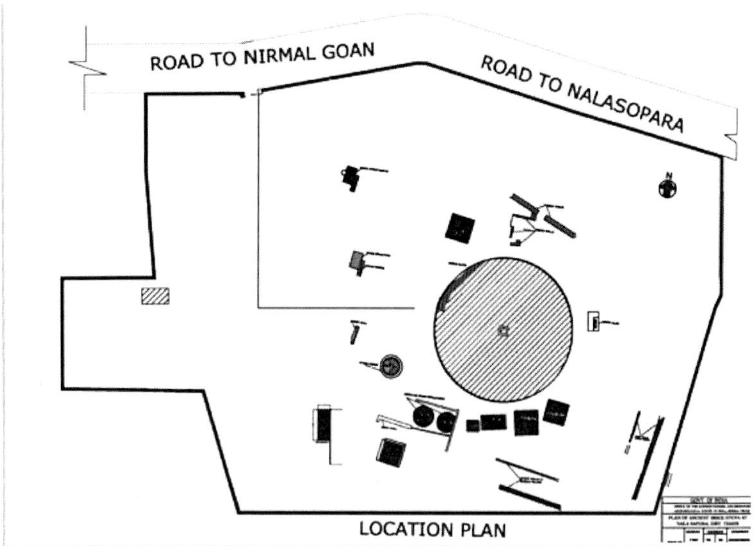

Fig. 20. Location plan showing main and votive stupas.

Index

Plates

Pl. 53: 1938-39 photograph of excavation around main tope of Nalasopara.

Pl. 54:-1938-39 photograph of excavation around main tope of Nalasopara.

Pl. 55:-1962 photograph of main tope (Stupa), Nalasopara.

Pl. 56:-1962 photograph of main tope (Stupa), Nalasopara.

Pl. 57:-1980 photograph of main tope (Stupa), Nalasopara.

Pl. 58:-1980 photograph of surroundings of main tope (Stupa), Nalasopara.

Pl. 59:-2010 Photograph of main tope (stupa), Nalasopara.

Pl. 60:-2010 Photograph of main tope (stupa), Nalasopara.

Pl. 61:-2010 Photograph of surroundings of main tope (stupa), Nalasopara.

Pl. 62:-During restoration of votive stupas around the of main tope (stupa), Nalasopara (2010-11).

Pl. 63:-During Scientific clearance of votive stupas around the main tope (stupa), Nalasopara (2010-11).

Pl.64:-During Scientific clearance of votive stupas around the main tope (stupa), Nalasopara (2010-11).

Pl. 65:-During Scientific clearance of votive stupas around the main tope (stupa), Nalasopara (2010-11).

Pl. 66:-During Scientific clearance of votive stupas around the main tope (stupa), Nalasopara (2010-11).

Pl. 67:-After restoration of votive stupas around the main tope (stupa), Nalasopara (2010-11).

Pl. 68:-After restoration of votive stupas around the main tope (stupa), Nalasopara (2011-12).

Pl. 69:-After restoration of votive stupas around the main tope (stupa), Nalasopara (2011-12).

Pl. 70:-After restoration of votive stupas around the main tope (stupa), Nalasopara (2011-12).

Pl. 71:-After restoration of votive stupas around the main tope (stupa), Nalasopara (2011-12).

Pl. 72:-After restoration of votive stupas around the main tope (stupa), Nalasopara (2011-12).

Pl. 73:-After restoration of votive stupas around the main tope (stupa), Nalasopara (2011-12).

Pl. 74 :-After restoration of votive stupas around the main tope (stupa), Nalasopara (2011-12).